From the Inside Out

A Forty-day Fast from Wrong Thinking

BY GREGORY DICKOW

GREGORY DICKOW MINISTRIES

THE POWER TO CHANGE TODAY!

P.O. Box 7000 • Chicago, Illinois 60680 • 888-849-5433 • www.gregorydickow.org

From the Inside Out by Gregory Dickow

Manuscript Compiled By
Ministry Solutions, LLC
P.O. Box 184
Mansfield, TX US
www.msicreative.com

ISBN-978-1-932833-13-3

TABLE OF CONTENTS

He performs wonders that cannot be fathomed, miracles that cannot be counted.
Job 5:9 (NIV)

INTRODUCTION

A LIFE-CHANGING JOURNEY

You are about to engage on an unprecedented journey, which has the remarkable possibility of changing your life forever. This devotional, *From the Inside Out*, is a uniquely-proven system, which will produce lasting results in your life. In essence, it is a forty-day fast from wrong thinking!

The way we think controls our entire life. Our thoughts shape our words, habits, and character. They have the power to produce life or death. Our thoughts release God's ability in our lives or limit us from experiencing His absolute best. The Bible says it best:

"For as he thinketh in his heart, so is he . . . ."

Proverbs 23:7 (KJV)

Before we begin this journey, let me lay some ground work and offer clarity concerning the concept of "fasting." Fasting is best described as "abstaining from something." We have often thought it only relates to food. And while fasting from food has its benefits, our focus here is something entirely different and powerfully refreshing. Over the next forty days, we will be fasting, or "giving up," wrong ways of thinking. This is the simplest and most effective form of fasting you will ever experience . . . and it works.

Jesus said to take His yoke upon you because it is *easy* and His burden is light (Matthew 11:30). He did the heavy lifting, and now your job is to enter into His rest. This is accomplished when you begin to believe and walk in the fullness of what God has already provided. That's what this kind of fasting is all about. You will be amazed at just how easy this will be: allowing the power of God to change you *From the Inside Out*!

One more thing to note: when your thoughts start to change, so will your conversation! It's a principle—"For out of the abundance of the heart, the mouth speaks," (Matthew 12:34, NKJV). Get ready for the words you speak to represent your new way of thinking, it's a powerful combination God has designed to produce lasting results in your life.

Let me encourage you to take a few minutes and write down whatever God puts on your heart after reading each daily thought. When you have completed the full forty days, you will be amazed at the things you have written and will see just how God has changed your thoughts and, consequently, your entire life!

It's time for us to take control of our lives by taking control of our thoughts. Too many people have lived below God's ultimate plan for their lives long enough! Today, that's all about to change, as we begin to walk in the victorious life God has intended.

I can tell you from my own experience and the amazing testimonies of others, that what follows on these pages will be the catalyst for a life beyond your greatest dreams! Are you ready to replace the wrong thoughts that have limited you with the unlimited possibilities of God?

Then let's go!

Gregory Dickow

DAY 1

"I CAN'T . . ."

There are so many things people think they CANNOT do. Everyday they are tormented by thoughts which say: "I can't change," "I can't believe," "I can't go on," "I can't make it," "I can't forgive," "I can't recover," "I can't accomplish my goals," "I can't find a job," "I can't find a spouse," "I can't go back to college," "I can't pay my bills," "I can't figure out my life," and the list is unending. This mentality and attitude sets you up to fail, to quit, and to live a negative, defeated existence. It is a poisonous thought of which you must no longer eat or drink.

Today, we are fasting from the thought, "I can't . . . ," and replacing it with, "I CAN . . . ." Philippians 4:13 says, "I can do all things through Him [Christ] which strengthens me." Henry Ford, one of the greatest innovators and mentors of our history, made this famous statement: "Think you can or think you can't. Either way, you will be right!" What does this mean? It sounds a lot like Proverbs 23:7, "As a man thinks, so is he," (paraphrased).

Remember this: *the Spirit of God lives on the inside of you!* This is an incredible truth because it means you CAN do what He CAN do in you and through you. 1 John 4:17 says, "As He is, so also are we in this world."

CHANGE IT TODAY

1. **Remember the little engine that could!** Over fifty years ago, the book called, *The Little Engine That Could*, spoke to a generation of children: "I think I can. I think I can. I think I can," AND IT DID!

2. **Say it: "I can!"** By simply saying this continually, your life will take the turn you desire.

3. **Fill your mind with God's Word:** Philippians 4:13, "I CAN DO all things through Christ who strengthens me," (NKJV).

4. **Get the words "I can't . . ." OUT of your vocabulary today.** Stop yourself every time you feel like saying it and let the new thought "I can," come out of your mouth. The more YOUR ears hear YOUR voice say this, the easier it becomes to believe it.

THINK IT & SAY IT

- I declare I can do all things through Jesus Christ who strengthens me.

- I eliminate "can't" from my vocabulary.

- I can do anything God's Word says I can do.

- I submit my thinking to the Word of God and my whole life is changing today.

POWER THOUGHT FOR TODAY

**Today is the first day of an incredible journey.
My life will never be the same for me!**

Day 2

"I don't have enough."

We have embarked upon a journey whose time has come. I have never been more excited nor expectant about anything of which I have been a part. Stay with me these forty days and watch what God will do in your life.

There is a mindset, an attitude, which says, "I don't have enough money," "I don't have enough time," "I don't have enough friends," "I don't have enough experience," "I don't have enough education," and so on. These thoughts are the invisible fences keeping people in the backyard of lack and insufficiency.

Our God calls Himself: *El Shaddai*—the God of more than enough! We have more than enough of God living inside of us! Change the thought of "not enough" to "more than enough!" Look at some references in the Bible where God proved Himself to be more than enough:

- In 1 Kings 17, there was more than enough for Elijah and the widow.

- In Exodus, there was more than enough for the children of Israel, *every day for forty years!*

- In John 6, there was more than enough bread left over after Jesus fed the five thousand.

In Mark 5, there was more than enough anointing for a demon-possessed man, the woman with the issue of blood, Jairus' daughter, and the people who were sitting by.

CHANGE IT TODAY

1. **Start believing you always have enough.** Philippians 4:19 says, "For my God shall supply ALL your needs according to His riches." Whenever we actually begin to believe this scripture, things start to change. This is not limited to money. It includes having enough time, enough opportunity, and enough of anything you need.

2. **Start thinking, "I always have enough."** My God is more than enough. He will open the windows of heaven and pour out a blessing that there will not be room enough to receive (Malachi 3:10). Luke 6:38 says He gives back to me good measure, pressed down, shaken together, and running over!

3. **Think of God's faithfulness.** David said, "I was young, and now I am old; and I have never seen the righteous forsaken or his descendants begging for bread," (Psalm 37:25, paraphrased).

4. **Fill your mind with this thought:** He is able to do exceedingly abundantly above and beyond all we can ask or think (Ephesians 3:20). He proved it by feeding five thousand till they were all full, and provided twelve baskets LEFT OVER!

THINK IT & SAY IT

- I will always have more than enough of whatever I need because God is my source. He provides me with enough money, time, energy, opportunities, or whatever is lacking.

- Because I think, "I have more than enough," it is easy for me to give. When I give for God's purposes, He will give to me good measure, pressed down, shaken together, and running over.

- God is faithful. He has never forsaken His descendants—and this includes me! He provided abundantly in the Old Testament and the New Testament. He is the same yesterday, today, and forever (Hebrews 13:8).

- I expect today for the needs in EVERY area of my life to be met and there to be plenty LEFT OVER!

POWER THOUGHT FOR TODAY

I will never again think: "not enough," because God is MORE than enough for me!

DAY 3

"I AM OVERWHELMED."

Welcome to our third day of fasting from wrong thinking. I want you to realize we are developing a habit. Do you know it only takes forty days (just six weeks) to establish a new routine? We're forming the habit of *abstaining* from negative thinking. Stay with it! You will be glad you did.

If you have ever felt overwhelmed, then today's thought is for you! Many times, people are burdened down with thoughts like: "This will take forever," "I've got too much to do," "This is too much for me to take," "There isn't enough time," or "I can't take it anymore." These thoughts have to go—today!

Think about this. Everything you see in this world was created by God in six short days. God is in the business of getting things accomplished, and getting them done fast. You can expect His help today and not have to carry your burden alone.

Most people don't understand what Jesus meant when He said, "Take My yoke upon you," (Matthew 11:29). A yoke is a harness or instrument placed upon two oxen. It causes them to plow together. So, when one gets weak or *overwhelmed*, he can continue by being pulled by the other. When we feel weighed down, we need to TAKE HIS YOKE. He is attached to us and will help carry the load. Of course, He ends up doing most of the carrying!

CHANGE IT TODAY

1. **Cast your cares upon Him.** He will care for you (1 Peter 5:7). How? Be honest. Tell Him what's wrong. Ask Him to carry it for you and believe He will. Remember, after you cast your cares, don't run to pick them up. Let Jesus carry the load for you.

2. **See yourself attached, or yoked, to Him.** He holds you up and pulls you when you are weak and overwhelmed.

3. **Begin to believe you can handle anything.** Start believing this *today*. You can handle and accomplish anything. Mark 9:23 says, "All things are possible to him who believes."

4. **Feast on this thought:** Nothing is too difficult for God. (Jeremiah 32:17). If nothing is too difficult for Him, and He lives in you—then nothing is too difficult for you!

THINK IT & SAY IT

- I can handle anything today, because I am yoked to Jesus. Today, I cast all my cares on Jesus. He cares for me and will carry my load.

- Nothing is too difficult for God, therefore, I declare that nothing is too difficult for me today! He is the author and finisher of my faith.

POWER THOUGHT FOR TODAY

**My success is determined by how I think.
I will think right and succeed!**

Day 4

"Something bad might happen to me or my family."

We are in day four of our fast from wrong thinking. Let me encourage you to keep eliminating toxic and poisonous thoughts which rob you from the victorious life you desire to live.

It is unfortunate we live in a society which is full of tragedy and suffering. News concerning violence, shootings, outbursts of deadly weather, and unexplainable disasters occur much too often. When things like this happen, it is easy for fear to creep in and make us think we are sitting ducks for Satan or twisted people to strike at any time.

DO NOT open the door to the expectation of evil! Your mind may argue with you, but that is why we're going to fast from this thought. Of course, *we must* have compassion, prayer, and practical support for those who have suffered; but we cannot allow what has happened to others to create our expectations and, consequently, live a life full of fear.

You're probably familiar with the Biblical account of Job's suffering and the tragic loss he experienced. What you might not know is one of the reasons this occurred: Job continually thought something bad might happen to his family. And just as he thought it would happen, it did. He said, "For the thing which I greatly feared is come upon me, and that which I was afraid of is come unto me," (Job 3:25, KJV).

Again, this confirms our foundational truth—as a man thinks within, so is he (Proverbs 23:7). Let's take this thought of fear and catastrophe captive today.

CHANGE IT TODAY

1. **Believe God's promise.** Psalm 91:10 says, "No evil shall befall you, nor will any plague come near your tent." The Message translation really brings this scripture to light: "Evil can't get close to you, harm can't get through the door." Then, in verse eleven, it goes on to say, "He ordered His angels to guard you wherever you go."

2. **Think within yourself: "No weapon formed against me shall prosper."** Isaiah 54:17 clearly tells us this. We will always have adversity, because we have an enemy. BUT, when we are attacked with the enemy's weapons, they are harmless and we are secure.

3. **Begin to speak the Word.** There is nothing stronger to combat the spirit of fear than you speaking the Word of God out of your mouth. Don't be like Job. Instead, fill your heart with God's promises of provision and protection.

4. **Know that God brings His Word to pass.** When we believe God's Word, then He has promised to bring it to pass. Jeremiah 1:12 says, "I am watching over My word to perform it." Everything God has spoken concerning you is being carefully attended to by God Himself. He will keep His promises and bring His Word to pass.

5. **Expect something good to happen to you and your family**. Whether you realize this or not, it takes as much energy to believe *bad things* are going to happen as it does to believe *good things* are coming your way. Start today and focus your thoughts and energy to believe God's goodness is yours, and good things are on the way!

THINK IT & SAY IT

- I believe the promises of God. Evil cannot come close to me.

- God guards me everywhere I go.

- I fill my heart and mouth with the good things God says about me.

- He is watching over His Word to perform it in my life; therefore, I expect something good to happen.

- My energy is spent on thinking and expecting good things to happen, and not bad!

POWER THOUGHT FOR TODAY

There is no stopping the man or woman who is set free from wrong thinking!

DAY 5

"I'M SO WORRIED."

Now that we are beginning to fast from wrong thoughts, we are developing a *habit of right thinking*. Not only are we overcoming each individual thought; but as we are consistent with this routine, we will reverse the tendency of thinking negatively into thinking positively. This is how we change *From the Inside Out*.

Worry not only has the power to weigh us down and depress us, but it also chokes out the Word of God which is sown in our heart. The key to fasting from this thought is to realize worry is a habit. The more you do it, the more you become addicted to it. People try to comfort themselves with worry, and yet it produces the exact opposite effect. We'll break this habit by fasting from the thought: "I'm so worried." How?

CHANGE IT TODAY

1. **Recognize worry does no good.** There is an old adage that is so true: "Worry is like a rocking chair. It gives you something to do, but it doesn't get you anywhere." Jesus said in Matthew 6:27-29, "Can all your worries add a single moment to your life? Of course not. And why worry about your clothes? Look at the lilies and how they grow. They don't work or make their clothing, yet Solomon in all his glory was not dressed as beautifully as they are,"

(NLT). If God can completely take care of the flowers of the field, then how much more is He able to provide *everything* you have need of?

2. **Recognize worry hurts.** It produces burdens and sickness. Proverbs 12:25 says, "Worry weighs a person down," (NLT). When something is hurting you, you'll usually stop doing it. Not only does worry bring damage to you, but also to those around you.

3. **Think about the good things in your life.** Worry is simply thinking about the things that are wrong or the things that *can* go wrong. So shift the focus to what's right in your life. Look what Psalm 103:2-5 says, "Forget none of His benefits; Who pardons all your iniquities; Who heals your diseases; Who redeems your life from the pit; Who crowns you with lovingkindness and compassion; Who satisfies your years with good things." Philippians 4:8 says to think on things which are true, honest, just, pure, lovely, and of a good report.

4. **Treat worry as a signal to pray.** Turn it around. Use worry as a weapon. It's telling you to pray! Philippians 4:6-7, "Don't worry about anything; instead, pray about everything; tell God your needs, and don't forget to thank Him for His answers. If you do this, then you will experience God's peace," (TLB).

5. **Focus on God's purpose for your life.** What is God's ultimate design for each of us? To win souls, serve others, and to be a blessing. Matthew 6:25 tells us not to worry about everyday life—whether you have enough food and drink, or enough clothes to wear. Isn't your life more than food and your body more than clothing? When you focus on fulfilling a purpose that serves God and others, worry leaves.

6. **Take a look outside.** Notice Jesus said in Matthew 6:28 to look at the birds, look at the lilies of the field, and look

at the grass. He wants us to look outside and notice His care over creation. The good news is this: YOU ARE THE CROWN OF HIS CREATION. Expect His care today!

THINK IT & SAY IT

- If God takes care of the flowers in the field, how much more will He take care of my needs? I'm not going to worry.

- I am no longer going to damage myself or those around me with thoughts of worry.

- God's benefits far outweigh my problems. I will focus on the good things God has done for me.

- When a thought of worry comes into my head, I use it as a sign to stop and pray.

- My focus is on doing the will of God—winning souls, serving others, and blessing people.

- God cares for me because I am the crown of His creation!

POWER THOUGHT FOR TODAY

**Thoughts are more powerful than devils.
Think right and I'll live right!**

DAY 6

"MY LIFE IS NOT AS GOOD AS OTHERS."

Too many times in life, people battle these thoughts of inferiority: "I'm not as well off as others," "I'm not as pretty," "I'm not as successful," "My life is not as easy or fun," or "Things always work out better for other people than for me." These types of thoughts lead to a major pity party and, eventually, to a life of depression. You never feel as if you can measure up to others and thus live below your own divine potential.

This is a deadly way of thinking which we are going to stop TODAY. Think about this: the very same people you think are better off than you may look at you the exact same way! You have no idea what goes on in the minds of others. But more importantly, you have the life God gave you, and nobody can be better at it than you.

Let's take these thoughts captive.

CHANGE IT TODAY

1. **Give up the temptation to compare yourself to others.** Society trains us to compare ourselves to one another, but 2 Corinthians 10:12 says when we do this, we are without understanding. Understanding is what gives us the power to be happy and free (Proverbs 3:13-19). Free yourself today from the comparison trap. Stop looking at someone else's money or figure, or your

friend's marriage and children. Get out of the pit where you think, "She's a better mom," or "He's a better dad." *When you compare, you despair.*

2. **Realize God has reserved a special gift for you.** There is a portion for you no one can take (1 Samuel 9:23-24). There is a life and assignment reserved just for you. The Bible says we all have different gifts—not competing gifts (Romans 12:6). Be happy with the gifts and life God has given you.

3. **Live your life to please God.** 2 Corinthians 5:9 says, "We have as our ambition . . . to be pleasing to God." When you are busy living to please Him, you no longer focus on what other people are experiencing or how you stack up against them. Stop living for the respect and esteem of others. He is not looking at how you compare to others; He is looking at whether you believe Him, trust Him, and honor Him. Colossians 3:1-2 says, "If then you have been raised up with Christ, keep seeking the things above, where Christ is, seated at the right hand of God. Set your mind on the things above, not on the things that are on earth." You see, we need to be eternally-minded.

4. **Personalize God's promises.** Whenever you see one of God's promises in the Bible just put your name in it! Learn to accept God is writing directly to you. Take for example Luke 12:32 which says, "*Your* Father, has chosen gladly to give *you* the Kingdom!" Personalize it: "*My* Heavenly Father has chosen gladly to give *me* the Kingdom!"

5. **Stop thinking backwards.** This means stop looking at what you *don't* have and start today looking at what you *do* have. You have eternal life. You are God's son or daughter. You are part of a spiritual family. You are part of a revolution—FROM THE INSIDE OUT! When you

think this way, you create an attitude of faith for all God has for you.

THINK IT & SAY IT

- I am secure. I have a special gift and treasure God has given me.

- There is a portion and a place in God's Kingdom reserved for me.

- All of God's promises are personally for me.

- I have a *great* life, because God is my Father and He has chosen gladly to give me His Kingdom.

POWER THOUGHT FOR TODAY

I am lacking nothing and therefore I am not jealous or envious of what anyone else has!

Day 7

"My life is not that significant."

We are one week into our fast now and forming the habit of abstaining from negative thinking is undoubtedly changing your world—and we are just getting started!

Before we look at today's thought, let me encourage you about something. As we address a particular thought, it's not unusual for it to come back to you. When it does, go back and re-read that particular page. Faith comes by hearing, and hearing, and hearing (Romans 10:17). Continue to attack those thoughts until it does not come back again. Now, let's move on to today's fast from wrong thinking.

Have you ever wondered, "What kind of difference can I make? I'm just one person. How can I be *that* significant?" The answer is quite simple: everybody can—and should—be making a difference in their world. To overcome this thought, you must come to realize and believe in your importance to God. Here are some fundamental reasons which will show you just how significant you are.

CHANGE IT TODAY

1. **You are God's highest creation.** Psalm 8:5-8 says, "Lord, you have made man a little lower than Elohim [God-Himself] and you have crowned him with glory and honor. You have made him to have dominion

over the works of Your hands; You have put all things under his feet, all sheep and oxen, even the beasts of the field, the birds of the air, and the fish of the sea that pass through the paths of the seas," (paraphrased). Take your rightful place as God's highest creation. See yourself as above and not beneath.

2. **He values you as much as He values Jesus.** The value of a thing is determined by how much someone would pay to purchase it. People will normally take better care of their cars than their tennis shoes. Why? Because the car costs more. God purchased YOU with His own Son—the ultimate price to pay! This brings your value up to the same level as Jesus!

3. **Jesus would have died for only you.** This thought is so humbling and magnificent at the same time. And yet, it is the absolute truth. Yes, Jesus did die for the sins of the world, but if it had just been for you, He would have paid the same price. This in and of itself makes you significant!

4. **You are His workmanship (Ephesians 2:10).** This is an amazing verse! The word "workmanship" is translated best as "a work of art." You're an original with no one else like you. You're not a copy. You are an individual work of art to God. See yourself as God's original masterpiece!

5. **You bring value to the Body of Christ.** Romans 12:4-5 says, "Just as each of us has one body with many members, and these members do not all have the same function, so in Christ we who are many form one body, and each member belongs to all the others," (NIV). Without you—your gifts, talents, and contributions—the entire Body of Christ suffers. We belong to Christ, and each one of us individually belongs to each other.

THINK IT & SAY IT

- I am significant. I bring value to those around me.

- I have a specific part in the Body of Christ. My life counts for something. The people in my life are better off because of my relationship with them. I am a work of art.

- I am the workmanship of God. You have made me a work of art. I am fearfully and wonderfully made, according to Psalm 139:14.

- I am the crown of Your creation. You provide for all my needs. If I was the only person on earth, You would have still sent Your Son to die on the cross. That makes me significant.

- I bless everyone I come in contact with today.

POWER THOUGHT FOR TODAY

I bring value to those around me and my life counts for something.

DAY 8

THE "GRASSHOPPER" MENTALITY

I want to build upon a thought from a couple of days ago, as I feel strongly about how this mindset must change in all of our lives. The "grasshopper" mentality might sound a little strange to you, but the thoughts which go with it are not foreign. Thoughts like: "I feel small," "I feel inferior," "My opposition is huge," "My problems are bigger than me," or "I'm not up for the challenge."

In Numbers 13, Moses sent out twelve spies to bring back a report on the land God had already promised to them. Ten spies returned with an evil report. They said, "We saw the giants in the land and we became like grasshoppers in *our own sight,* and so we were like grasshoppers in their sight." Listen to their report! They became in others' minds what they were in their own minds.

The longer they focused on their opposition, the bigger their opposition became. Soon, their faith in the God who had brought them out of the bondage of Egypt was swallowed up. With it, went their ability to believe they could indeed conquer and possess the land. *Others saw them the way they saw themselves.*

Let's change the way we see ourselves starting today! Let's discover what God says about us.

CHANGE IT TODAY

1. **We are royalty!** Royalty destroys inferiority. Romans 5:17 says through the gift of righteousness, we reign as kings in *this* life. When you know you are in God's royal family, you will no longer feel inferior or think like a grasshopper. We have received the gift of righteousness (2 Corinthians 5:21), therefore we are kings. We are royalty!

2. **We live life from His position and His seat.** Ephesians 2:6 says, "He raised us up with Him, and seated us with Him in the heavenly places, in Christ Jesus." There is no higher place to be than seated with Jesus in heavenly places. This is our rightful position. We live from here and reign in this life seated next to our King, Jesus.

3. **We are made in His image.** Genesis 1:26 says we are made in the very image and likeness of God. We have His divine image, with His divine breath, and are endowed with His divine authority. When you look at yourself in the mirror, you are looking at the image of God!

4. **We are not judged by man.** This doesn't mean we avoid accountability or responsibility, but it means we are inferior to no one. Paul said in 2 Corinthians 11:5, "For I consider myself *not* in the least *inferior* to the most eminent apostles." He was talking about his peers. Colossians 2:16 warns us, "Let no man therefore judge you," (KJV). Critical, jealous, insecure people can make you feel real insignificant very quickly.

5. **We are masters over our life.** Romans 6:14 says, "For sin shall not be master over you." Luke 10:19 says we have authority over all the power of the enemy, so the devil is not our master either. God has given us the ability to rule and reign over our lives, our emotions, and our self-image. One of the revealing names given to Jesus

by His disciples was "Master." "Master" means *"one who controls or influences events or things."* When He healed the sick, they called Him Master. When He calmed the storm or forgave the unforgivable, they again called Him Master. He was Master over life and circumstances. According to 1 John 4:17, "As He is, so also are we in this world."

THINK IT & SAY IT

- I am not inferior to anything or anyone, because I am made in the image of God.

- I am the righteousness of God, and therefore I reign in this life as a king in God's Kingdom.

- I am in the royal family, and *royalty destroys inferiority*. I have His divine image, His divine breath, and I am endowed with His divine authority.

- I am as He is—in *this* life. I am not under man's opinion and judgment. I am only under God's.

- I am seated with Christ in heavenly places, and therefore I see myself from His point of view. I am bigger than the mountains, taller than the trees, and more a giant than the giants! No "grasshopper" mentality lives in my head any longer. I shall, by all means, go up and take possession of the Promised Land!

POWER THOUGHT FOR TODAY

Royalty destroys inferiority!

DAY 9

"WHAT'S WRONG WITH ME?"

Have you ever thought this? Sure you have. Who hasn't? We have all had our bouts with sin-consciousness—a haunting awareness of all we do wrong and all that is wrong about us. The first problem with this thinking is it is "me-centered," not "Jesus-centered." It's selfish. We are called to *look* to Him, "the author and finisher of our faith," (Hebrews 12:2, KJV). God instructs us to look *up*, not look *within*.

Another problem with this thinking is it's *too obvious!* There are many things wrong with all of us. We are a flawed people from a natural point of view, but not in God's eyes. Thinking, "What's wrong with me?" breeds perfectionism, self-centeredness, obsessive introspection, and condemnation for our flaws and shortcomings. Of course, we do need to admit our mistakes and weaknesses and receive God's forgiveness and strength. But don't make this your focus in life.

We are going to crush this thinking today!

It starts with developing a "righteous-consciousness" rather than a "sin-consciousness." The constant awareness of our "falling short" is where the devil and religion want us to live. This keeps us defeated and limited; hemmed in by our human nature, rather than liberated through our divine nature. 2 Peter 1:4 says through His promises, we share in the divine nature of God and escape the corruption that is in the world through lust. Look at how God has designed us to live and, more importantly, to think.

CHANGE IT TODAY

1. **Understand the gift of righteousness.** 2 Corinthians 5:21 says, "He made Him who knew *no* sin, to be sin on *our behalf*, that we might *become* the righteousness of God in Him." This is the greatest exchange in human history! Jesus took our sinfulness and imparted to us His righteousness, which means we are *right* in God's eyes, not wrong. We are justified. I like the play on words here. Justified = "just-if-I'd" never sinned.

2. **Awake to righteousness.** 1 Corinthians 15:34 says, "Awaken to what's right in your life." You are a child of God, a joint heir with Jesus Christ (Romans 8:17). You are forgiven. When God looks at you, He sees the blood Jesus shed. He sees His Son. When God thinks of you, He thinks of a victorious, conquering, strong, powerful, wise, and holy son or daughter. He sees you as a mighty champion, the head and not the tail (Deuteronomy 28:13). "Righteousness" means *"to stand in the presence of God as if sin had never existed."* We can now stand in His presence without any sense of guilt, shame, inferiority, or condemnation.

3. **Eliminate sin-consciousness.** When you are always conscious of what's wrong, you will *do* wrong. When you are always conscious of being the righteousness of God, you will *do* right. Your actions on the outside will reflect how you see yourself on the inside. Whenever you think of your "wrongs," cast them upon Jesus. And remember, His "rights" are now yours!

4. **Ask the Holy Spirit to do what He does best.** 1 Corinthians 2:12 says, "Now we have received, not the spirit of the world, but the Spirit who is from God, that we

might know the things freely given to us by God." When you live in sin-consciousness, you think the Holy Spirit is only revealing all that is wrong in your life. Not true! The Holy Spirit's key ministry is to reveal what is already yours.

THINK IT & SAY IT

- I decide to give up thinking about all that is wrong in my life, and I choose to think about what is right.

- I am the righteousness of God, through the blood of Jesus. I stand in the presence of God without guilt, shame, inferiority, or condemnation.

- I awake to what's right and believe it will lead me to a victorious life.

- I am a joint heir with Jesus. When God looks at me, He sees His blood. He thinks of me as a conquering, powerful, and holy son or daughter.

- I will not think of myself as anything less—or more—than what God thinks of me!

Fasting from wrong thinking is releasing supernatural power into your life. These simple strategies are helping you overcome the destructive thought patterns which have produced defeat and lack.

POWER THOUGHT FOR TODAY

The seeds of right thinking will produce great harvests in every area of my life.

DAY 10

"THAT'S JUST THE WAY I AM."

One of the things which limits and keeps us defeated is the opinion we have of ourselves. Over time, what other people think—or more importantly, what they say—about us begins to shape our view of ourselves and what we are capable of accomplishing. People's opinions will condition us to live up—or down—to their expectations.

Throughout your life, maybe you have heard things like, "He's shy," "She's so stuck up," "He's all talk," or "She's not the sharpest knife in the drawer." When we are surrounded by these, and other comments, it produces negative, limiting thoughts inside of us. We feel, "I'll always be average," "I'll always be overweight," "I'm capable of only making a certain amount of money." We are always limited by our self-imposed expectations.

Today, we are breaking out of the limitations and boundaries we, or others, have put on us. This may have been the way you were, but it's not the way you *are*.

CHANGE IT TODAY

1. **God is the potter; we are the clay.** Jeremiah 18:1-6 gives a beautiful description of how God is in complete control of our lives. It portrays God as the potter, someone who is skilled and patient, and us as the clay.

rom the Inside Out

He is molding us into the person He has designed us to be. Trust the Artist to make a masterpiece. Be flexible and adaptable. See yourself as a *good* work in progress.

2. **Don't pre-judge your capacity.** Philippians 1:6 says, "He who began a good work in you will perfect it until the day of Christ Jesus." Withhold judgment of yourself or others. Only God knows what your full potential is. Let Him reveal it to you today.

3. **God never gives up on you.** In comparing us to the clay, Jeremiah 18:4 says, "The clay was marred in the hand of the potter: so He made it again," (KJV). It doesn't matter if you have not lived a flawless, perfect life—and who has? God doesn't throw you out and will continue to develop you into the best you can be.

4. **You are changing daily.** Whatever flaws you have, they are not the final sentence. You are *now*, daily being conformed to the image of Jesus (Romans 8:29)!

THINK IT & SAY IT:

- I am unlimited in my ability to grow and change.
- I am what God says I am.
- God began a good work in me, and He will finish it.
- I am not in bondage to my weaknesses.
- Every day and every moment which passes is making me more and more like Him.

POWER THOUGHT FOR TODAY

I am His workmanship—His work of art!

DAY 11

"DON'T GET YOUR HOPES UP."

After only ten days, you are certainly starting to see a pattern of positive, Biblical thinking replacing negative unbiblical thinking. That's exactly what this fast is designed to do—replace long-believed lies with the truth. Thought patterns shape our expectations and our actions. Like a magnet, our thought life "attracts" the things which fill our minds.

Today's thought, "Don't get your hopes up," has subtly found its way into our heads. We have been trained by doubt and unbelief to lower our expectations and to brace ourselves for mediocrity and the status quo. To "hope" is to look up, to have expectation! To "hope" is to live. Hope is like oxygen. It's like light in a dark and negative world.

It has often been said man can live forty days without food, four days without water, four minutes without oxygen, *but not four seconds without hope*. Proverbs 13:12 says, "Hope deferred makes the heart sick." When hope is put off to the side, or dashed to the ground, your heart becomes sick. Most importantly, your heart becomes sick when you *stop* hoping. **Hope is a healer of the heart.**

CHANGE IT TODAY

1. **Get your hopes up.** No matter what, you can always have hope! Psalm 78:7 says, "That they might set their hope in God."

2. **Keep your hopes up.** 1 John 3:3 says when you fix your hope on Him, you are then purified.

3. **When you don't see something happening, hope even more.** The fact that you don't see it, gives hope a reason to remain alive in your heart. Once you obtain something, you don't need to hope for it any longer. You already have it. It's when you don't see it, that your hope has a reason to exist.

4. **Get faith.** Faith is not like hope. Faith cannot be delayed. Faith is a tangible force and a substance. If you are exercising faith, no one will be able to tell you God's promises will not come to pass. All fear and doubt passes away, and you will be thoroughly convinced of God's promise in your life. There are no ups and downs, just a knowing and a sense of His presence. Faith will overcome all opposition. Faith is the fulfillment of your hope—it is the tree of life.

5. **Meditate on the love of God.** Hope that is not deferred, delayed or disappointed, comes from love—God's love in you. Romans 5:5 says, "And hope does not disappoint [*or leave you with shame*], because the love of God has been poured out within our hearts."

6. **Free yourself from negative people.** There are people who think they're doing you a favor by "managing" your expectations or "protecting" you from disappointment. Get around people who are full of hope and can dream with you. These types of relationships will encourage you to live in your highest expectation!

THINK IT & SAY IT

- My hopes are up! I eliminate the notion of lowering my expectations.

- I refuse to accept people's advice to "not get my hopes up." I get my hopes up NOW, and I will keep them up.

- I expect God's promises to come to pass in my life today. I expect good to come to my life today—in my family, my home, my church, on my job, in my relationships, in my body, and in my finances.

- I expect ideas, favor, and wisdom to come to me. I look up, expecting to receive the best of what God has for me today.

POWER THOUGHT FOR TODAY

Because of God's promises, I have unlimited and unhindered hope and expectation.

DAY 12

"I'M NOT SMART ENOUGH."

This deceptive mindset permeates our thinking and keeps us limited in what we can do and what influence we can have. It's another tool the devil uses to try and make us feel inferior.

Most media and institutions of "higher learning" are not as smart as they think. Just look at how the media reports on politics, world events, or the economy. They try to sound so smart, but I don't think they even understand what they're saying half of the time!

This world's system is designed to make us feel like we don't know enough about what's going on, so we will be dependent on the information they provide.

Think about this: if you are born-again, you are brilliant! The Bible says *you have the mind of Christ* (1 Corinthians 2:16). His mind is far smarter than the smartest business professionals, educators, politicians, and newsmakers combined. And now, you have His mind in you!

CHANGE IT TODAY

1. **Dwell on the fact that you have the mind of Christ.** You have the ability to see things the way God sees, understand the way He understands, and choose the way He would choose. Stop listening to any thought otherwise.

2. **Expect God's wisdom today.** James 1:5-6 says, "If any of you lacks wisdom, let him ask of God who gives to all men generously. . . . But let him ask in faith without doubting." God's wisdom is available for you and is just one prayer away. When you ask for wisdom, God will provide it.

3. **You are constantly learning.** Psalm 16:7 is an incredible verse which says, "My mind instructs me in the night." Friend, you are so smart that your mind is even teaching you while you're sleeping!

4. **Stop trying to measure up.** If you ever feel foolish or less educated than the mentally "elite," God has a great answer for you: He takes the foolish things of this world to confound, or shame, the wise (1 Corinthians 1:27).

5. **Don't think small anymore.** As well, don't talk small. You are made in the image of God with His intelligence, His brilliance, and His understanding. Think of yourself this way; talk this way and you will see yourself this way.

THINK IT & SPEAK IT

- I have the mind of Christ. I think His thoughts and understand His ways! I make wise and intelligent decisions.

- I will never again submit to the thought of, "I'm not that smart," or "I can't figure it out." I *am* smart and I *can* figure it out.

- I expect wisdom today and I expect *my mind to instruct me in the night!*

- I make wise and intelligent decisions.

- I will never again be intimidated by the mentally "elite."

- I will never again think small again. I was made in the image of a BIG God, and now I think BIG thoughts!

POWER THOUGHT FOR TODAY

I am made in His image and am filled with His intelligence, His brilliance, and His understanding.

DAY 13

THE "VICTIM" MENTALITY

When you fast from food, it affects your whole day. In the same manner, we need this fast from wrong thinking to be a part of our entire day. Joshua 1:8 says as you meditate on the Word day and night, wherever you go you'll prosper and whatever you do will be blessed. That's because the creative power and energy of God is cultivated and released in the soil of your thought life.

Remember, our lives don't improve through external changes. We change from the inside out. *"As a man thinks within, so is he!"* (Proverbs 23:7).

Today, we're fasting from a "victim" mentality. Too many people live under the mental attacks which say, "It's someone else's fault," "I was mistreated," "If someone gave me a break, I could make it, too," "It's the government's fault," "It's how I grew up," "It's not my fault," . . . and so on.

Viktor Frankl, who survived a Nazi death camp at Auschwitz, defined ultimate freedom as *"the ability to choose one's attitude in any given set of circumstances, to choose one's own way."* The worst prison in the world is the one we put ourselves in—our mind. A victim mentality cripples our ability to grow and strips us of the power God has given us to live victoriously.

A victim mentality is a thought we need to completely dismantle.

CHANGE IT TODAY

1. **Begin to take responsibility.** No one can keep you in your current situation, except you. Begin today to accept total responsibility to become a victor, not a victim.

2. **Understand what responsibility means.** The root word of "responsibility" is "response." You may not be able to control everything others do to you, but you can control your *response*. In your response lies your freedom and your growth!

3. **Don't stay where you are.** People may have had something to do with how you got into a certain situation, but only *you* can decide whether you stay in those circumstances or begin to live above them.

4. **Stop the "victim" mentality.** Begin to take full responsibility for your attitude and direction in life. Deuteronomy 30:15,19 says, "See, I have set before you today life and prosperity, death and adversity. . . . So choose life, that both you and your descendants might LIVE [the victorious, abundant, God-kind of life]."

5. **Ask the Holy Spirit to help you.** Taking full responsibility doesn't mean you're in it alone. God is on your side and He will help you. It's natural to look for help, but get it from God. John 16:7 says the Holy Spirit is "our Helper"! When you have His help, you don't need to blame anyone for anything! You blame when you're helpless—*but you are not helpless!*

6. **Don't give away your power.** When you allow others to determine how you respond, you give away the power to live in victory, health, and success. You have the power to choose, the power to forgive, the power to recover, and the power to overcome anything. When you blame others, you give away that power to them.

7. **Take charge of what God has given you.** The master said to the servant who hid his talent, "Why didn't you at least invest my money so I could have received interest?" (see Matthew 25:24-27). He blamed the master and excused himself. As a result, he fell to the temptation of resentment and fear. He lost everything because he had a victim mentality. Be a good steward of the things God has provided for you.

THINK IT & SAY IT

- No one can keep me down. I am not a victim. I am a victor. I take full responsibility for my responses in life—my attitudes and my decisions.

- God has set before me prosperity or adversity. He has given me the power to choose. I choose prosperity!

- Holy Spirit, I am asking for Your help. You live in me, and You are my Helper!

- I refuse to give away my power by blaming others. I choose to respond to life with God's Word.

- I take responsibility for my thoughts, my actions, and my REACTIONS. I abandon the idea that my situation is the fault of anyone else.

POWER THOUGHT FOR TODAY

I am an overcomer. I am more than a conqueror through God's great love.

DAY 14

"IT'S NO USE."

There are some other thoughts which accompany this one. Thoughts like: "I might as well give up," or "It just doesn't work for me." These are mentalities which will defeat you. Some people think this way until it becomes a disease. We "dis-ease" ourselves with defeatist thinking. Winners don't think like this. People don't want this kind of spirit around them.

Overcoming this mindset is simple.

CHANGE IT TODAY

1. **Get into a partnership with God**. This is the only place where you cannot fail. Psalm 124:2 says that the Lord is on your side! This is not religion. This is common sense. You cannot fail when you awaken to the fact He walks with you!

2. **Recognize the problem exists for you to conquer.** Sometimes things go wrong in life. Perhaps it's a job loss, a financial hardship, or a difficult relationship. Numbers 13:30 says, "We should by all means go up and possess the land, and conquer it," (paraphrased). Find the "means." Find the source of the problem and conquer it!

3. **Get understanding.** Proverbs 3:15 says, "She [*understanding*] is more precious than jewels; and

nothing you desire compares to her." Ask for understanding, and God will always give it. Evaluate what you have and put it to good use!

4. **Start believing that it DOES work for you!** It works for anyone. Remember, Jesus said in Mark 11:23, "*Whoever* says to this mountain, 'Be taken up and cast into the sea,' and does not doubt in his heart, but believes that what he says is going to happen, it shall be granted him." Think this marvelous promise; believe this marvelous promise!

5. **Stop waiting for opportunity to come.** Stop thinking you don't have the opportunities others have. Fight the fight of faith and don't *give up* until opportunity shows up! Do it regardless of your feelings.

THINK IT & SPEAK IT

- I give up giving up.

- I am in partnership with God. He is on my side; therefore, I cannot fail.

- My problems don't devour me. I eat them for lunch! I have the spirit of might and power.

- I will conquer my problems in every way and by every means. God gives me understanding, which is true wealth.

- Things DO work out for me. They work out for whosoever believes! I'm a believer, not a doubter.

- Opportunity comes to me, because I expect it to.

POWER THOUGHT FOR TODAY

I will not waiver, give up, or quit until God-ordained opportunities come to me!

DAY 15

"I HAVE TO SETTLE WITH WHAT I HAVE."

To "settle" means to accept something which is not ideal or desirable, just because you don't believe it could be any better. Many people settle for less than God's best in their life. Their relationship with the Lord can get better, but they don't think it can, and so it doesn't progress. This mindset is destructive because it accepts life the way it is rather than making it the way you want it to be.

There is a story found in John chapter five, which tells of a lame man who settled by the pool of Bethesda for thirty-eight years. He had accepted the thought he would never get better; that he would never get the help he needed to be healed. He was discouraged and beaten *until* Jesus showed up in his life and showed him he didn't have to settle—and neither do you!

Let's take control over this thought today and live life to the full!

CHANGE IT TODAY

1. **Desire.** Jesus said in essence, "You have to want it!" Get desire back in your life. Desire to improve. Desire to get better. Desire to make something great of your life.

2. **Stop making excuses.** "No one helps me," "No one understands," "No one gives me a break," "I was just meant to suffer in this way." Shut those thoughts up!

The lame man said, "I have no man to help me," (John 5:7, NIV). Stop making excuses and start living!

3. **Do something *now* to make things better.** Improve yourself. Learn something new. Take a class. Learn a new language or an instrument. Don't let life dictate to you that "this is all there is."

4. **Believe in the God who is able.** The Bible says God "is able to do exceeding abundantly beyond all that we ask or think," (Ephesians 3:20). Believe He is able to do this for you.

5. **Don't settle for less than God's best.** Don't settle for sickness. Don't settle for just getting by. Don't settle for the way things are. In Mark 10:46-52, blind Bartimaeus would not settle for his current condition. He cried out to Jesus and was healed. Refuse to accept anything less than God's best for your life!

THINK IT & SAY IT

- I will never again settle for a mediocre, average existence.

- I will not settle for things the way they are. There is more to this life God has for me. I expect Him to do exceeding abundantly beyond all I can ask or think.

- I will think big and ask big. Then, I will experience BIG!

POWER THOUGHT FOR TODAY

Jesus came to give me life—abundant in quantity and superior in quality.

DAY 16

"WHATEVER HAPPENS MUST BE GOD'S WILL."

D o you realize your life is changing for the better, just as the Bible said it would? We are being *transformed* by the renewing of our minds and we are coming into the perfect will of God.

Yesterday, we continued our fast from wrong thinking by eliminating the thought: "I have to settle with what I have." Today, I want to build upon this. Many times, our mind (and the devil) tells us if things don't go our way, then it must be God's will. I do realize many people reading this know *theologically* God's will is for good. But, when we face resistance or it seems like God is not responding, we're tempted to give up and let whatever happens happen.

Not anymore—after today!

If there ever was a story in which best illustrates how to change this mindset, it is the story of blind Bartimaeus. When he heard Jesus had the power to heal, he began to cry out, "Jesus, have mercy on me!" (Mark 10:46-52). Many people told him to be quiet, but he cried out even more. He refused to accept this condition as God's will. Neither should we!

CHANGE IT TODAY

1. **Stop listening to voices trying to keep you the way you are.** There are voices in your head saying, "Keep quiet." There are voices from others saying, "Stay the way you are." There are voices saying, "God must not want you to have this." NO. NO. NO. NO. NO. Shut those voices up and listen to the voices of faith and possibility!

2. **When you face resistance, add persistence!** In verse forty-eight, when people tried to shut Bartimaeus up, he cried out *even more*. Press through until you receive your promise!

3. **Don't give up.** When Jesus heard Bartimaeus crying out, *He stood still*. (Now I'm preaching here!) Don't give up or move away until you have Jesus' attention. When your persistence causes Jesus to stop and notice you, your miracle is on its way!

4. **Believe God wants to fulfill your desires, not just your needs.** In verse 51, Jesus said, "What do you *want* Me to do for you?" Truthfully, Bartimaeus could have lived without sight, but Jesus asked him what he *wanted*, not just what he *needed*. God doesn't just meet our needs. He fulfills our desires—provided that our desires are founded on Scriptural promises (Psalms 37:4).

5. **Make up your mind that you will not be denied.** Bartimaeus would not be denied. The woman with the issue of blood would not be denied (Mark 5:25-34). The four men who were determined to get their friend to Jesus would not be denied (Mark 2:4). You and I will not be denied.

THINK IT & SAY IT

- I decide today that I will stop listening to the voices telling me to stay the way I am.

- I will not be quiet when asking God to fulfill His promises. My prayers will not be silenced by doubt, fear, or opposition.

- I believe God wants to give me the desires of my heart and not just my needs.

- When I face resistance, I will add persistence.

- I will not give up or give in to my present condition.

- I will press through the opposition and will not be denied.

POWER THOUGHT FOR TODAY

I will not tolerate a present condition of discouragement, sickness, poverty, or mediocrity— NOT ANOTHER DAY OF MY LIFE.

DAY 17

"I AM LIMITED BY MY FINANCIAL STATUS."

I know as you replace this wrong thinking with right thinking, you are going to see things change quickly in your finances and in your peace of mind! Today, we are dealing with what I call a "limitation mentality." This is the mindset which always says, "You are limited," "You never have enough," and "If you only had more money, you could be happy or do more for God."

All those thoughts actually keep us from doing more and from being happy. Let's take some steps to remove this thinking of limitation.

CHANGE IT TODAY:

1. **Be happy now.** Happy is the man who fears the Lord (Psalm 112:1). When you *think* you need more to be happy, you program yourself to stay unhappy until you have more. This is a dangerous attitude. The truth is, when you are grateful for what you have, you will become magnetic to more. More will come.

2. **Recognize God is not limited by money**. Since this is true, neither do you need this restriction. You are made in God's image. He fed the children of Israel with manna from heaven (Exodus 16:15). He commanded water out of a rock (Numbers 20:11). He sent a raven to feed Elijah

(1 Kings 17:4-6) and sent a prominent family to take care of Elisha (2 Kings 4:8).

3. **Believe in the God of ideas.** Proverbs 8 says God will give us witty inventions. These are creative ideas. When God opens up the windows of heaven, He is raining ideas—not $100 bills. When Jesus needed bread, He multiplied the five loaves He had been given (Mark 6:37-42). When He needed tax money, He got it out of a fish's mouth (Matthew 17:24-27). When He needed wine, He used water (John 2:1-10). Expect the heavens to open with angelic intervention, wisdom, ideas, hope, words of knowledge, and much more.

4. **Get wisdom.** When offered one request from God, Solomon asked for wisdom (2 Chronicles 1:7-12). God was so impressed, He gave Solomon wisdom—and with it came wealth, power, and answers. James 1:5 says, "If any man lacks wisdom, let him ask of God who gives to ALL men generously," (paraphrased).

5. **Don't underestimate the power of imagination.** We are to cast down "imaginations" which exalt themselves above the knowledge of God (2 Corinthians 10:5). But, God-given imagination is a *must*. Ephesians 3:20 says that He is able to do exceedingly abundantly above and beyond all that you can ask, think, or imagine! Note, the emphasis on: "YOU CAN ASK, THINK, OR IMAGINE." You CAN and you MUST imagine!

6. **Be provision-conscious not need-conscious.** Make up your mind to expect that God will provide. Put your thoughts on His generosity and provision, rather than on what you need or don't have. Every time we give something valuable to God, we prove we are provision-conscious, not need-conscious.

THINK IT & SAY IT

- I fear, reverence, and respect God; therefore, I am happy now.

- My present happiness will attract more of what I need into my life.

- God can work in my life regardless of my financial status. He is not limited by money; therefore, neither am I.

- I believe God is a God of ideas; therefore, I expect ideas to come to me. Ideas are worth more than money. I will be a vessel of God-given ideas.

- I think wisdom and ask for wisdom. God richly supplies me with wisdom every time I ask for it.

- I will ask, think, and imagine what God can do, and He will exceed my expectations and imaginations!

- I do believe the heavens will open over my life. I choose to be provision-conscious, rather than need-conscious.

POWER THOUGHT FOR TODAY

By changing the way I think, I am becoming a magnet, which attracts God's provision for my life.

DAY 18

"IF I ONLY HAD THE RIGHT SURROUNDINGS . . ."

Many people believe if their surroundings were better—they just moved to a different city, had a better boss, or if someone gave them a chance—they would prosper and succeed. *Nonsense!* They use these thoughts as excuses for why things don't get better or why they don't reach their goals and improve their life. This way of thinking makes people blame others and their circumstances for why they don't change.

Do you want to succeed in any circumstance? Then, let's fast from this wrong way of thinking!

CHANGE IT TODAY

1. **It's not what surrounds you, but what's inside you which brings success!** 2 Corinthians 4:16 says, "Therefore we do not lose heart, but though our outer man is decaying, yet our inner man is being renewed day by day." Notice, Paul is saying that even when things go wrong on the outside, deal with the inside! *This is a vital key to success.* And what does God say we should do on the inside? Be renewed, day by day. Absorb these scriptures day by day, and the INSIDE will overtake the OUTSIDE!

2. **Success or failure in life is created by how you think.** Joshua 1:8 says, "But you shall meditate on the Word of God day and night . . . for then *you will make* your way prosperous, and then you will have good success," (paraphrased). I want you to notice something very powerful here. The Bible says that **YOU** shall make your way prosperous, not God! Don't wait for God to do it. He's waiting for you to change the way you think.

3. **Understand the source of blessing.** Psalm 1:1-3 says, "Blessed is the man that does not walk in the counsel of the ungodly . . . . he meditates on the Word day and night. He will be like a tree firmly planted by streams of water, whose leaf does not wither, who bears fruit in his season, and whatever he does, prospers," (paraphrased).

4. **The root to true success is a prosperous soul.** 3 John 2 says, "Beloved, I wish above all things that you would prosper and be in health, even as your soul prospers," (KJV, paraphrased). When your soul is prospering, your entire life is prospering.

5. **True success is: the presence of God.** Look at the life of Joseph. He was thrown into a pit by his brothers and sold into slavery. Genesis 39:2 says, *"And the LORD was with Joseph*, so he became a successful man."* Notice, even though his surroundings were terrible, *he still became a successful man.* He had bad breaks and was surrounded by bad people, yet still succeeded BECAUSE GOD WAS WITH HIM!

6. **Create your surroundings.** We create our breaks by the thoughts we think and the choices we make. Deuteronomy 30:15,19 says, "See, I have set before you today life and prosperity, and death and adversity . . . choose life!" You can create your own environment by making the right decisions.

THINK IT & SAY IT

- I am being renewed on the inside by the Word of God, which will bring success in every area of my life.

- My success is created by how I think. I agree with God's thoughts and meditate on God's Word day and night.

- Success follows me. I prosper in my soul—in my mind. I fill my mind with the richness of God's Word, and therefore it spills over into every area of my life.

- Like Joseph, I will not allow my negative circumstances to determine my success or failure. *I am a successful and prosperous man or woman* because God is with me.

- I create positive surroundings and I create good breaks by choosing life today!

POWER THOUGHT FOR TODAY

It's not what surrounds me BUT WHAT'S INSIDE ME that determines my success!

DAY 19

"PROSPERITY IS DEFINED BY WHAT I HAVE."

Over the past couple of days, we have focused on fasting from wrong thinking where success is concerned. And the truth is, success or failure in life is created by how we think.

Many people equate prosperity only with money. This is wrong thinking. True prosperity is not what you have. It is who you are—on the inside! The prosperity God emphasizes is the *prosperity of our soul*. 3 John 2 says, "Beloved, I wish above all things that you would prosper and be in health, even as your SOUL PROSPERS," (KJV). As our soul goes, so goes every area of our life. Therefore, true success or prosperity means taking care of our soul.

Jesus said it this way, "For what does it profit a man to gain the whole world, and forfeit his soul?" (Mark 8:36). In the pursuit of "gain" many people forget to take care of their soul. This is the key to real success.

Let's take a look at several things which will make your soul prosperous and in turn, bless every other area of your life.

CHANGE IT TODAY

1. **Meditate on the Word of God**. There are many verses in the Bible which talk about finances, and you need to know them. However, learn to meditate on the riches

that are yours in Christ—not just financial riches, but also "soul" riches such as wisdom, grace, peace, and righteousness. Your soul will begin to prosper, and then your outside will catch up with your inside.

The great missionary Hudson Taylor was approached by his wife on the mission field when they were out of money. "What is left, Hudson?" she asked. "We have twenty-five cents, dear," he responded, *"and all the promises of God."* Hudson Taylor understood true prosperity.

2. **Develop a righteousness consciousness.** This step is irreplaceable. Fill your mind with the blessings which come from being the righteousness of God. In Acts 13:10, the devil is called "the enemy of all righteousness." He opposes righteousness because it is what changes us. When we awake to righteousness, we will sin not (1 Corinthians 15:34).

3. **Have confidence in the love of God.** In Mark 1:11, God says, "You are my beloved," (NKJV). He is saying that to you right now. He loves you astronomically more than any parent could ever love his or her child. And that's saying a lot!

4. **Develop covenant relationships.** This term is often misunderstood. It means connecting with people of like mind and spirit, who are going in the same direction as you are with God. I gladly extend my covenant with you. When we have the strength of covenant partnership we will be able to handle anything—this is success and prosperity.

5. **Don't take things personally.** This is one of the great forces of "soul-poverty." When you become the victim in someone else's drama, your soul becomes poor. Clear your heart and mind of what is called "people guilt." This is where you carry around the responsibility for how

everyone feels toward you. You don't have to be the "host" of anyone's pity party!

6. **Stop comparing yourself to others.** This will rob your soul of prosperity, as you languish in what you don't have, rather than meditating on what you do have. 2 Corinthians 10:12 says that we are without understanding and without happiness when we compare ourselves to others.

THINK IT & SAY IT

- I am blessed with the wisdom of God, the grace of God, and the righteousness of God.

- I have all the promises of God—which makes my soul prosper.

- God loves me and is on my side; therefore I am satisfied by His love.

- I open myself to covenant relationships which will bring strength and blessing to me and those I am in covenant partnership with.

- I refuse to take things personally. I will not absorb people's guilt or manipulation.

- I choose to stop comparing myself to others. This robs my soul of its health and well-being.

POWER THOUGHT FOR TODAY

**True prosperity is not what I have —
it's who I am in Christ!**

DAY 20

"I JUST CAN'T HOLD IT ALL TOGETHER."

This thought can be paralyzing. It gets you thinking about how hard things are, how many things depend on you, and the possibility of everything falling apart.

How many of us think this way about our jobs, daily responsibilities, or our emotions? How about our families, kids, and all the activities: school, sports, and extracurricular stuff?

Thoughts feed expectations. Expectations feed into manifestations. Manifestations become imprinted in our minds, forming our habits and character, which is our consistent patterns of behavior.

This is why it is vital to FAST from WRONG THINKING and replace wrong thoughts with right ones. Let's do it.

CHANGE IT TODAY

1. **Make a decision.** Let's go back to Philippians 4:13 which says, "I **can do all things** through Him [Christ] which strengthens me." The way to turn this thought into a reality is through the decision to believe it. DECISION is the doorway into reality. We take a wrong thought captive by bullying it with the right thought. Make this new thought PRESS against the wrong one until there's no room in your head for the wrong one.

2. **Realize you are not alone**. You are not in this by yourself! Fill your mind with this thought from Hebrews 13:5 where God said He would never desert you, nor forsake you. Combat the thought of, "I can't hold it together," with "I'm not doing this by myself. God is with me and He will never leave me alone!" Whether you are a single parent or a single person, God is in this with you—married or divorced. Whether you are struggling financially or the wealthiest person alive, He is with you in your struggle and daily responsibilities.

3. **God holds together the things we turn over to Him.** 2 Timothy 1:12 says, "I am persuaded that He is able to keep [hold together] that which I have committed unto Him," (KJV). You see, whatever we COMMIT to Him, He will keep, guard, and hold together for us. If there is an area of your life which seems like it's falling apart, COMMIT it to Him, and He will get involved.

4. **Fill your mind with this thought: The Lord will accomplish that which concerns me.** Psalm 138:8 says He will accomplish, complete, and perfect everything concerning you. He will get involved with the things that concern you and will add His grace to your situation!

5. **God upholds the universe with His Word.** If His Word can keep the whole universe together, then it can definitely hold your stuff together! Make God's Word the base and foundation of everything you think, every decision you make, and everything you do.

THINK IT & SAY IT

- Even when I feel I can't keep it all together, I declare that I can do all things through Christ. He gives me the strength I need, when I don't have enough.

- I decide to believe in His strength. I am strong in the Lord and in the power of His might.

- I am not alone, because He will never leave me nor forsake me.

- I am a victor and not a victim. I have committed my life, my body, my family, and my money to God; therefore, He will hold together the things I have committed to Him.

- He is, even now, involved with and accomplishing those things which concern or trouble me.

- His Word upholds the universe; therefore, I will think, believe and speak His Word throughout my day. It is *more than enough* to hold my world together.

POWER THOUGHT FOR TODAY

**My new thought life is reshaping my entire life.
I am changing daily from the inside out.**

DAY 21

"THERE'S JUST NO WAY! THERE'S NOTHING I CAN DO ABOUT MY SITUATION."

We've all thought this at times. Sometimes we feel we've blown it or we're at the end of our rope. We think there's nothing we can do, but it's a lie. There's always something we can do. There's always a way.

Friend, the devil would love for you to believe there's nothing you can do about your situation. He wants you stuck! He wants you immobilized. He wants you defeated. He achieves this by getting us to believe this lie.

This way of thinking keeps you from being decisive and taking action. Action produces results. But thinking you can't do anything about your situation or that you don't know what to do about it, paralyzes you from taking action.

Today, we are fasting from thinking, "No way!" and replacing it with, "*I think and believe there is always a way,*" even when it seems like there is none. John 14:6 says, "I am the way, and the truth, and the life." Jesus is the Way when there is no way. He is your way out of whatever situation you are experiencing. EXPECT HIM to make a way.

CHANGE IT TODAY

1. **Trust the ministry of the Holy Spirit.** This can happen in your everyday life. Romans 8:26 says, "We don't

always know how to pray as we should, but the Spirit intercedes for us," (paraphrased). No matter what your situation, the Holy Spirit knows how to bring about God's will for your life as you pray and worship Him.

2. **Think this thought today: PRAYER CHANGES THINGS.** There's nothing you can't impact with prayer. Prayer gets you unstuck. It gets you moving again toward victory. Never see prayer as something that is weak. It is powerful! "And *all things*, whatsoever you shall ask in prayer, believing, *you shall receive,*" (Matthew 21:22, KJV paraphrased).

3. **Believe that FAITH FINDS A WAY.** In Mark 2:1-5, the four friends of the paralyzed man could not find a way into the house where Jesus was. They were stuck. BUT, THEY BELIEVED THERE WAS SOMETHING THEY COULD DO ABOUT THE SITUATION. By believing there was a way, they found one! They went up on the roof and lowered him down through the ceiling tiles and the man was healed. Why? Because faith found a way! When we don't think it, we don't look for it.

4. **Expect God to make a way.** When it seemed like the three Hebrew men in Daniel chapter 3 were going to be burned in the fiery furnace, Jesus showed up. What was an impossible situation was made possible because Jesus was with them. *And He is with you* in your fire. Expect God to make a way.

5. **Stop thinking you have to figure it all out right away.** When you feel stuck, just take one step forward. When Jesus was tempted to back down and not go to the cross, the Bible says He went forward a little (see Mark 14:35). When you feel paralyzed—like there's nothing you can do—just take a step. Don't think about all the steps. Just take the first one. In a relationship, the first step may be to say that you're sorry. If it's finances, maybe just cut one area of spending or give one extra offering. If it's in

your health, take the first step and have a salad. Just take that one little step!

THINK IT & SAY IT:

- I believe in the ministry of the Holy Spirit to intercede for me when things aren't working out. He will work through the situation to bring about God's will. He will bring me through.

- As I pray, I believe things will change; they will improve. I walk by faith, not by sight and faith finds a way.

- I think and believe there is always a way even when it seems like there is none. Jesus is the Way when there is no way.

- He is with me no matter what fire or situation I encounter. I expect Him to make a way for me.

We are at the end of our third week! Your life is changing daily, *From the Inside Out.* Keep up the great work. Stay faithful to our fast from wrong thinking. There is so much more coming your way!

POWER THOUGHT FOR TODAY

Today I will take the one step which will move me toward healing, blessing, and God's will for my life.

DAY 22

"IT'S TOO LATE."

O ur society is so "time conscious." We allow time to limit us, define what we are capable of achieving, and what God can do in our lives.

It's engrained in us to think it's too late to change; to start a new career; to save a marriage; to recover from a major mistake; to start over again; to be forgiven; or even too late to have a second chance.

The truth is: IT'S NEVER TOO LATE! When you realize it's not too late, you have hope. You take action. You move forward. You stop thinking that it's futile and useless to do the right thing.

CHANGE IT TODAY

1. **Un-decide it's too late for things to change**. Un-decide you can't recover! Un-decide the damage is irreversible.

2. **Meditate on the fact that God created time**. He can multiply it for you. The earth and sun stood still in Joshua 10:12-13, "And Joshua spoke to the Lord . . . and said in the sight of Israel, 'O Sun, stand still at Gibeon, and O moon in the valley of Aijalon.' So the sun stood still, and the moon stopped." Joshua had control over time for God's purpose. Start thinking this way: you are not controlled by time; but by God's grace, you control it!

3. **Think about the great cloud of witnesses**. It wasn't too late for Abraham to father a child at ninety-nine years of age or Sarah to be a mother at ninety. It wasn't too late for Peter after he denied the Lord three times. It wasn't too late for Paul, who persecuted and murdered Christians. In business, Ray Kroc started the first McDonald's when he was fifty-six years old!

4. **Dwell on God's mercy and grace**. Lamentations 3:23 says that God's mercies are new every morning. Hebrews 4:16 says, "Come boldly to the throne of grace to receive mercy and grace in your time of need," (NKJV, paraphrased). "Mercy" is when God doesn't give you the judgment you DO deserve. "Grace" is when God gives you the goodness you DON'T deserve.

5. **Stop making excuses for why it's too late.** God doesn't listen to our excuses. Actually, *He ignores our excuses* and expects us to believe in His faithfulness. Moses wasn't confident due to his speech impediment. But he was given chance after chance to be used by God and to deliver His people. Remember 2 Timothy 2:13, "If we are faithless, He remains faithful; for He cannot deny Himself."

6. **Ask God for more time or a second chance.** When Hezekiah turned back to the Lord and asked for a second chance, God told him, "I have heard your prayer. I have seen your tears; surely I will heal you. . . . And I will add to your days FIFTEEN YEARS," (2 Kings 20:5-6). If he did it for Hezekiah, He will do it for you!

THINK IT & SAY IT

- I believe it's not too late for things to improve in my life and radically turn around.

- God created time and He can multiply it for me. I am

not controlled by time, I control it! God's grace is sufficient for me.

- It wasn't too late for Abraham, Sarah, Peter, or Paul. *It's not too late for me*!

- I stop making excuses but choose to believe in His faithfulness. He gives me mercy and grace in my time of need.

- God is no respecter of persons. If He multiplied time back for Joshua and Hezekiah, He will do it for me!

POWER THOUGHT FOR TODAY

It's not too late for me to recover from a tragedy or mistake, to turn my life around, to take better care of myself, to apologize to someone, to forgive, to surrender my life to God, to change the way I see myself, and to have a new beginning!

DAY 23

"IT'S NOT WORKING."

People think, "I'm trying, but I'm not really changing," "My marriage is not working," "Prayer is not working," "My budget is not working," "The Word is not working," "Tithing isn't working."

When things don't go our way, we tend to think the good we're doing is not accomplishing anything. The devil gets us thinking God's Word works for others but not us. When we believe, "It's not working," we adopt a mindset which blocks us from continuing to do the right thing—and that's when we lose our harvest. You see, it's not that it's not working, but we've stopped "working it," which halts our progress.

When we do the right thing, the devil loves to get us to think it didn't do any good, and nothing will change. When we forgive someone, the devil says, "That didn't do any good." When we give an offering, the devil says, "You won't get a harvest." When we pray, we hear the thought telling us, "God didn't hear me," or "He won't answer that."

When my kids were little, I would sometimes wonder, "Is praying over them every night working? Is disciplining them working? Are the kisses and hugs and long talks working?" But I kept doing it because I thought, "God's Word is true and it works." Today, my four oldest children are all teenagers who love God, love their parents, and love each other. I now realize it was working all along. If I would have thought, "It's not working," and would have stopped acting on the Word, this thought would have defeated me.

Today, we turn the tables on these thoughts.

CHANGE IT TODAY

1. **Keep sowing the right seeds.** The Bible instructs us not to grow weary while we are doing good. It tells us that in due season, we will reap if we do not give up (see Galatians 6:9). We need to believe that if we don't give up, we will get our harvest.

2. **Understand that growing weary, fainting, and giving up, begins in our minds.** Hebrews 12:3 says, "For consider Him who has endured such hostility by sinners against Himself, so that you may not grow weary and lose heart [or faint in your minds]." Giving up starts in your head. As soon as we think it's not working, our bodies respond to those thoughts, producing negative energy. In your mind, you have to start thinking, "It is working!" and then positive, life-filled energy is produced.

3. **Believe God is at work in you right now.** He is all the while "at work in you, both to will and work for His good pleasure," (Philippians 2:13). If He is working in you, things are going to work.

4. **Let this penetrate your thinking: the Word works!** Jeremiah 1:12 says, "I am watching over My Word to perform it." Believe in the integrity of God's Word.

5. **Believe that prayer works.** Jesus said, "Whatever things you ask [or desire] when you pray, believe that you receive them, and you will have them," (Mark 11:24, NKJV).

6. **Don't let immediate feelings or appearances trick you.** Things start to work the moment you act on the Word of God. 2 Corinthians 5:7 says, "For we walk by faith, not by sight," (NKJV).

7. **Remember, it's going to work out, if you trust and let God's timing come to pass.** God's Word says He makes all things beautiful in His time (Ecclesiastes 3:11).

THINK IT & SAY IT

- Things are working. I may not see them right now, but God says they are at work.

- I am sowing the right thoughts; therefore, my life is changing. I am sowing the Word of God, and it will not return void.

- I will not give up in my mind. I make up my mind to believe it is working.

- God is at work in me, and He is bringing His will to pass in my life as I surrender my thoughts to Him. As I sow the Word of God in my heart and mind, God is watching over His Word to bring it pass.

- Whenever I think prayer doesn't work, I will replace that thought with Mark 11:24.

- I walk by faith—by believing what God says.

- I will not allow the appearance of something to trick me into thinking God's Word is not working.

POWER THOUGHT FOR TODAY

The Lord is making things beautiful in my life, no matter what they look like right now.

DAY 24

"YOU NEVER KNOW WHAT THE FUTURE HOLDS."

There are several thoughts which go along with this particular mindset. Things like, "You never know what's going to happen," "You can't control what happens in your life," and "There's not much I can do about it." Too many people relinquish their power and authority to do something about their situation. We think it is all up to God or our future is predestined. It is true we cannot control everything that happens in the world, but we *can* control what happens in our lives.

Here is a foundational pattern to remember: our thoughts produce our actions. Our actions produce our habits. Our habits produce our character. Our character shapes our destiny. You see, we do have the power to create the future we desire . . . and it all begins with how we think!

Let's change the thought from, "You never know what the future holds," to "I hold the future in my hands, based on the seeds I sow."

CHANGE IT TODAY

1. **Believe what God said.** Jeremiah 29:11 says that God's plan for us is for good and not evil. He promises us a *future* and a *hope*. God's future for us is good. Expect it today!

2. **Your life is a garden.** Genesis 2:8 talks about how God put man in the garden. But in Luke 17:21, God put the "garden" IN MAN. Jesus said, "The kingdom of God is within you," (NKJV). In Matthew 13:19, Jesus said that the Kingdom of God is in our hearts.

3. **You determine your future by the seed you sow.** Galatians 6:7 says, "Do not be deceived . . . whatever a man sows, is exactly what he will reap," (paraphrased). We need to sow the seed of God's Word. The Word is a seed. Promises from God's Word contain the power to come to pass when they are planted in the fertile soil of our heart (see Mark 4).

4. **God gives you permission to grow whatever life you want.** Proverbs 4:23 instructs us to watch over our heart with all diligence, for out of it flow the issues of life. Jesus said, "Whatever you loose on earth, will be loosed in heaven," (Matthew 16:19, NKJV). This means whatever we allow, heaven allows. God allows you to create the abundant life He has promised.

5. **You are in control of the things which can choke out your desired harvest.** Mark 4:13-20 says there are three things which can choke out the harvest of God's Word in our lives: the desire for other things, the deceitfulness of riches, and worry (which we dealt with on Day 5).

6. **Desire God's promises in your life.** 2 Corinthians 1:20 says, "For all the promises of God in Him are yes," (NKJV). Sow the seed of God's promises in your life. The answer is YES!

7. **Meditate on the power God has given you.** God has given you the power to choose (Deuteronomy 30:19), the power of your seed (Galatians 6:7), the power of your tongue (Proverbs 18:21), and the power of the Holy Spirit in your life (Acts 1:8).

THINK IT & SAY IT

- I accept in my heart and mind that God has a good future in store for me.

- God has given me the stewardship over the garden of my heart. I will watch what goes into my heart through my eyes, ears, and mouth.

- I determine my own future by the seeds I sow.

- The Word of God contains the seeds of God's promises. God has given me permission and the power to sow it into my heart.

- I don't need to desire other things, since there are so many promises of God to feast upon. I recognize and activate the power of choice, the power of my seed, the power of my tongue, and the power of the Holy Spirit.

POWER THOUGHT FOR TODAY

The promises of God for me are "YES!" They will come to pass as I plant them in my heart!

DAY 25

"IF I LIVE RIGHT, I WILL GET CLOSER TO GOD."

I want to bring your attention to the fact that some of the thoughts we need to fast from and eliminate from our heads *seem* like "right" thoughts. But, in reality, they are subtle tricks and lies.

When the devil approached Adam and Eve in Genesis chapter three, it says he was subtle—more so than any other creature. It's these subtle thoughts that defeat us. They seem so "godly" and so "right," but they are not right. They produce a "works" mentality and a legalistic approach to our relationship with God.

I don't want to create a theological debate here, but I do want to ask you a question. How much closer can God get than to live inside of you? 2 Corinthians 13:5 says, "Do you not recognize this about yourselves, that Christ Jesus is in you?" Our bodies are the temple of God (1 Corinthians 6:19).

This is not a warning to be afraid of; this is a promise. It's a fact when a person is born again. It is a picture of how there is no separation between us and God. Paul is, in essence, saying (and I am praying you will receive this with an open heart), "The reason your behavior has been sinful and negative is because you have lacked the knowledge that He lives in you. When you realize this, it will change how you look at yourself, and it will then change how you live."

When we think we have to *do more* to get closer to God, the focus is put on us. When you buy into this thought, you try so hard to get close to God. Then you get discouraged, until you either give up or assume your relationship with God will always be distant. This affects your peace, your joy, and—of course—your confidence in prayer. But Hebrews 12:2 says we have to fix our eyes on Jesus, not ourselves.

It is what I call an "illusion of separation." The devil—and even religion—has caused us to think God is far off: "He's way up there, and we're way down here. But, if we pray enough, fast often enough, and do enough, then we can close the gap and get Him to come closer." That is a lie. He is the friend who sticks closer than a brother (Proverbs 18:24).

This is a thought we must deal with—NOW!

CHANGE IT TODAY

1. **You don't earn closeness with God.** It is a gift. Hebrews 13:5 says, "I will never leave you nor forsake you," (NKJV).

2. **You are already in His presence by the blood of Jesus.** Hebrews 10:19 says, "We have confidence to enter into the Holy place by the blood of Jesus."

3. **There is no separation between you and God.** When you are born again, you are united with Him and one with Him. 1 Corinthians 6:17 says, "But he who unites himself with the Lord is one with Him in spirit," (NIV). Acts 17:28, says, "'For in Him we live and move and have our being,'" (NIV). This is the reality the early Christians had and lived by. There is no separation. Yes, sin separated us from God, but Jesus removed sin and reconnected us to God. Now, there is no separation.

4. **Stop thinking, "He's there, and I'm here."** You don't have to do something to get God into your situation. He is already in it, because you're in it. The Bible says He is at work in you to bring about His good pleasure (Philippians 2:13).

5. **Fear no evil.** Psalm 23:4 says, "Even though I walk through the valley of the shadow of death, I fear no evil; for Thou art with me."

6. **Reject the lie that God is "out there" somewhere.** Reject the lie that your answer or blessing is "out there" somewhere. The Bible says those who hear the Word and accept it, will bear fruit (see Mark 4:20). You have to accept this truth. There is no separation.

THINK IT & SAY IT

- I am not separated from God anymore. I don't have to earn closeness with Him; it is a gift. He will never leave me nor forsake me.

- I stop thinking that "He is there, and I am here." He is in my life and my situation right now. No matter what I walk through, I am not afraid for God is with me.

- I reject the lie that He is out there somewhere. I accept that there is no separation between God and me. Romans 8:38-39 says that nothing can separate me from the love of God!

POWER THOUGHT FOR TODAY

**I am in God's presence and He is in me.
In Him, I live and move and have my being.
I live in this reality.**

DAY 26

"GOD IS FAR FROM ME."

I really want to build upon what we dealt with yesterday. Remember, the serpent was subtle in Genesis chapter three. Thoughts which can defeat us are often very subtle thoughts. We have to learn to not only discern between right and wrong, but we must discern between right and "almost right."

It's "almost right" to ask God to come down and help us. It sounds holy. It sounds humble. But, you will only be truly free when you discover, He is already here. "Emmanuel" means "God with us." When Jesus came to the earth, He put an end to the separation between God and Man. God is not only with us and for us; God is also *in us.*

This is an amazing mystery, and we won't understand it completely until we are in heaven. Colossians 1:27 says, "This mystery, which is Christ in you, the hope of glory," (NIV).

It's "almost right" to believe if we become holier, we can get closer to God. But separation between us and God is a myth. It is an illusion. The devil wants us to believe it to keep us powerless and misinformed concerning our connection with God. It is true Isaiah 59:2 says, "But your iniquities [or sins] have made a separation between you and your God," but Jesus took away the sin through His blood. Therefore, there is no separation between us and God if we have been born again. Our failure to recognize that keeps us in bondage and feeling distant from God. Sometimes we feel He is so far away, but He's not. He is here. He is there.

Let's replace this "almost right" thinking with right thinking.

CHANGE IT TODAY

1. **REALIZE He is present with you RIGHT NOW.** The Bible says God is an ever-present help in times of trouble (Psalm 46:1). WOW! You have to love this thought. Have you ever had times of trouble? (Haven't we all?) But notice, it says He is *ever-present*. Then it says, "help in times of trouble." It is His "ever-presence" that brings us help in times of trouble. Ask the Holy Spirit to help you today!

2. **Take Him at His Word.** Jesus said in Matthew 28:20, "Lo, I am with you always; even to the end of the age," (NKJV). There is no way to misinterpret this verse. "I am with you always." This truth has to warm your heart and comfort you.

3. **Acknowledge that Christianity is not a life of attainment, but a life of recognition.** Philemon verse 6 says, "Your faith may become effective by the acknowledgement of every good thing which is in you, in Christ Jesus," (NKJV). Many people focus on "attaining" God's presence and God's blessing. But the Scripture is clear: we must recognize and acknowledge He is already in us. His gifts are already in us. This produces power money and religion cannot buy! The first part of the verse says this is what makes your faith become effective. Acknowledge. Recognize. He is already in you. His gifts are in you.

4. **Remember Christianity is not us "finding God."** He came and found us, took us into His arms, spilled His

blood to cleanse us from all unrighteousness, and breathed His very Spirit into us. Now, He lives in every person who has accepted Jesus Christ as their Lord. Romans 8:11 says, "But if the Spirit of Him who raised Jesus from the dead dwells in you, He who raised Christ from the dead will also give life to your mortal bodies through His Spirit who dwells in you," (NKJV).

5. **Eliminate every thought which says, "God, come down and help me," or "Send Your Spirit."** He has already come. He has already sent His Spirit. Our fight, our battle is to believe this whether we "feel" His presence or not. He is in you!

6. **See yourself as inseparable from God!** David said in Psalm 139:7-10, "Where can I go from Your Spirit? Or where can I flee from Your presence? If I ascend to the heavens, you are there; if I make my bed in Sheol, you are there. If I take the wings of the dawn, if I dwell in the remotest part of the sea, even there your hand will lead me, and your right hand will hold me," (paraphrased).

THINK IT & SAY IT

- I decide today to eliminate the thought: "I am separated from God in any way."

- God is an ever-present help in my time of trouble. His ever-presence brings me help! He is in my boat and I will rest in knowing I am in His presence.

- I recognize God is already in me. That's what makes my faith work. He has found me and put His Spirit in me. The very same Spirit which raised Jesus from the dead is living on the inside of me.

- God is not far off. He is right here, right now. I am surrounded by His love and enveloped in His presence; therefore, I am not afraid.

- God is my shield and my refuge, my fortress and my very present help today.

- I am not trying to live for God; I am living from Him. His power is in me. His presence is in me. His love is in me.

POWER THOUGHT FOR TODAY

Nothing can ever separate me from the love of God which is in Christ Jesus my Lord!

DAY 27

"WHERE IS GOD WHEN I NEED HIM MOST?"

We are continuing to distinguish between "right" and "almost right" thinking! There are many things we have believed which are "almost right." It's "almost right" to believe if we worship God with all our heart, we can usher ourselves into the presence of God. Many ministers will even say, "Let's press into His presence." But you see, we are already in His presence, because we have passed through the veil which separated us from the holy of holies. It is through the body and blood of Jesus that we pass through the veil (see Hebrews 10:19-20).

We now stand in His presence unashamed, without guilt, without condemnation, and without separation!

When the disciples tried to cross over to the other side of the sea in the boat (see Mark 4:36-40), they were overwhelmed by the storm which struck their ship. They feared for their lives and, bailing out water furiously, surely thought they would die. Have you ever been in a storm? The waters crashing against you and you don't know what to do. You feel helpless. You cry out, "Lord, where are You? Don't You care?"

The disciples forgot one small detail in the midst of their storm—Jesus was in the boat with them! There was nothing greater than His presence!

Let's overcome the thought that says, "I'm alone in this storm."

CHANGE IT TODAY:

1. **Recognize He is in the boat with you!** In Mark 4:36-40, Jesus was asleep in the boat. Someone asked me once, "How do we wake Jesus up when He is asleep in our boat in the middle of a storm?" I said, "Well, you don't wake Him up; you rest with Him!" **If He's not worried, then you don't need to worry!** His presence calmed the storm then, just as it will now.

2. **Wake up to the fact that God is with you.** The disciples didn't need Jesus to awake. They needed to **AWAKEN** to the fact God was with them; therefore, there was nothing to fear. When you know He is with you, there is nothing to fear. Psalm 23:4 says, "Though I walk through the valley of the shadow of death, I will fear no evil; for You are with me," (NKJV).

3. **You can have peace in the midst of your storm.** Great miracle: Jesus calmed the storm. Greater miracle: Jesus slept in the midst of it. When you realize He is in your boat with you, you will have a supernatural peace. Calming the storm is great; but peace *in the midst of it, is greater!*

4. **Do not mistake fire in your life for God's absence.** In Daniel 3:22-25, Jesus was the fourth man in the fire with Shadrach, Meshach, and Abednego. His presence was felt in the middle of the fire. Just because you don't feel His presence, doesn't mean He isn't there with you. Believe He is with you, and eventually your situation will feel and respond to His presence!

5. **You have His mightiest Angel at your side!** Psalm 34:7 says, "The Angel of the LORD encamps around those

who fear Him, and rescues them." Now, there are many angels in our lives, but this is talking about *the* Angel of the Lord. The Old Testament "Angel" is Jesus Christ. He will deliver you and rescue you in your time of need.

THINK IT & SAY IT

- There is nothing greater than God's presence, and His presence is with me and in me.

- I do not have to try to "get in" God's presence. I am already there through the blood of Jesus.

- He is in my boat with me. He is not "over there." He is "here" right now, with me and in me!

- I will awake to the fact He is with me. There is no separation.

- I am fearless, because He is with me and encamped around me; therefore, no evil shall befall me, nor shall any plague come near my dwelling place—my church, my home, my body, and my life—in Jesus' Name.

POWER THOUGHT FOR TODAY

**I can rest with Him in the midst of any storm.
I can walk with Him in the midst
of the fire.**

DAY 28

"IT'S SO HARD!"

Many people don't even start some things because they have conditioned themselves to think it's too hard. This thought paralyzes us into moving forward or taking risks.

Life has its challenges for all of us, but it's not too hard when we live it the way God has designed. Nothing works right when we don't follow the manufacturer's specs or instructions. Life is too hard for Christians who try to live their lives apart from God. When you get born again, the God of "possibility" lives in you!

As we fast from wrong thinking today, let's take a refreshing and renewed look at how life was meant to be lived.

CHANGE IT TODAY

1. **Realize you are yoked to Jesus.** Many people find the Christian life so difficult because they are trying to do it on their own. The Christian life was not meant to be lived this way. We were meant to be yoked to Jesus. He said, "Take My yoke upon you. For My yoke is easy, and My burden is light," (Matthew 11:29-30).

2. **Trust that His grace is sufficient for you (see 2 Corinthians 12:9).** Accept the fact that some things are difficult in our own strength, but know God wouldn't ask

us to do something He doesn't give us the strength to do. 1 Corinthians 10:13 says, "And God is faithful, who will not allow you to be tempted beyond what you are able, but with the temptation will provide the way of escape also, that you will be able to endure it." Expect His grace and divine ability in your life today.

3. **Mediate on the fact that you are one with Him.** 2 Corinthians 13:5 says, "Do you not recognize . . . that Jesus Christ is in you?" He is in you. So, whatever you are facing, He is facing with you. Your problem is His problem. Your trial is His trial. Your debt is His debt and He will *never* let you down.

4. **Think on God's nature, His ability.** Jeremiah 32:17 says, "Ah, Lord GOD! Behold, You have made the heavens and the earth by Your great power and by Your outstretched arm! Nothing is too difficult for You," (paraphrased). The Message translation says, "Dear God, my Master, you created earth and sky by your great power—by merely stretching out your arm! There is nothing you can't do!"

5. **Remember Matthew 19:26: "With God all things are possible."** You see, what is impossible and too hard for Man, is easy for God. The God of the impossible lives in you.

6 **Don't focus on doing things "for Jesus," but "from Jesus."** Galatians 2:20 says, "It is no longer I who live, but Christ lives in me; and the life which I now live in the flesh I live by faith in the Son of God, who loved me and gave Himself for me," (NKJV). Trust His power to live through you!

THINK IT & SAY IT

- I am not alone in the challenges and responsibilities of my life.

- I am yoked to Jesus. His yoke is easy and His burden is light.

- The Holy Spirit is my Helper. He lives in me and gives me His strength, encouragement, and power.

- God knows what I'm going through and He has given me the grace and ability to make it.

- I have a covenant with God; therefore, my battles are His battles.

- I live life from the strength He supplies in me.

- I can do all things through Christ who infuses me with His strength!

POWER THOUGHT FOR TODAY

Nothing is too difficult for God and all things are possible for me, because I believe.

DAY 29

"GOD IS MAD AT ME."

Many people think God is mad at them or they think bad things happen because God is against them. Perhaps you don't think He's overtly against you, but He's just not aggressively helping you either. These thoughts are designed by the devil and your flesh to undermine your faith. If you think God is mad at you, then you won't be expectant toward God to bless you.

In Deuteronomy 1:26-27, the children of Israel fearfully complained about their trials. They said, "It's because the LORD HATES US, that He has left us here to die in the wilderness," (paraphrased). Notice, their mentality: they actually thought and said, "The Lord hates us." This led to their failure in the wilderness. Our belief about God's love will lead us to success in our trials and daily lives, just as their belief that He hated them led to their failure. BELIEVE THE LOVE HE HAS FOR YOU TODAY!

Let's take this thinking captive. The word "captive" means *"to conquer with a sword."* You conquer wrong thinking with the sword of God's Word!

CHANGE IT TODAY

1. **God is not mad AT you. He is mad ABOUT you!** This is something I started saying when I began our ministry fifteen years ago, and I will never stop believing it! When

you accept this thought, you will have confidence, expectation, and peace. We can all use that! How do I know this is true? Romans 8:38-39 says that nothing can separate you from the love of God. You are forgiven (see 1 John 1:9) and you are loved (see John 15:9).

2. **Think this new thought: God loves me as much as He loves Jesus!** In John 17:23 Jesus says to the Father, "I in them and You in Me, that they may be perfected in unity, that the world may know that You sent Me, and loved them, as much as you have loved me," (paraphrased). What an amazing truth! God loves you as much as He loves Jesus, and there is no way God can be mad at Jesus.

3. **Understand God thinks precious thoughts about you all the time!** Psalm 139:17-18 says, "How precious are Your thoughts toward me, O God! . . . If I should count them, they would outnumber the sand. When I awake, I am still with you," (paraphrased).

4. **Whatever God said to Jesus, He says to you, too.** "You are My beloved Son, in [You] whom I am well-pleased," (Mark 1:11). Hallelujah! He doesn't sound mad at Jesus! He sounds "mad about Him!" 1 John 4:17 says, "As He is, so are we," (NKJV). Look, there is no getting around this marvelous truth: God doesn't love Jesus half-heartedly; therefore, He doesn't love you half-heartedly either. He sees you just as He sees Jesus!

5. **Realize God is holding nothing back from you!** Romans 8:32 says, "He who did not spare His own Son, but delivered Him up for us all, how will He not also with Him freely *give us all things*!"

6. **Understand you are not condemned!** Romans 8:1 says, "There is now no condemnation for those who are in Christ Jesus." Condemnation is an expression of strong disapproval. God approves of you because of

your faith in Jesus, not because you have done everything right. God's love for you is non-negotiable. Jeremiah 31:3 says that He loves you with an everlasting love. It cannot be stopped, quenched, or compromised.

THINK IT & SAY IT

- God is not mad at me; *He is mad about me.*

- God loves me as much as He loves Jesus. I am His beloved and He is mine!

- There is nothing God is holding back from me. He didn't hold back His best; therefore, He won't hold back the rest!

- I refuse to be condemned. I am forgiven. I reject the thought that He is mad at me or against me. I believe God loves me! I believe the love He has for me will always lead me to success and victory. For LOVE never fails!

POWER THOUGHT FOR TODAY

God is for me and not against me. His love toward me cannot be stopped, quenched, or compromised.

DAY 30

"GOD IS JUDGING ME."

We all feel at times like we don't measure up and perhaps God is mad at us. When something goes wrong, it's easy to think, "Why is God doing this to me? Why is this happening to me?" This kind of thinking distorts the true view of our Heavenly Father. We need to stop seeing God as a vengeful and judgmental God. He is just, but His justice was satisfied through the shed blood of Jesus. All that's left is His mercy and grace.

We have begun to replace this wrong thinking with the thought: "God is not mad *at* me; He is mad *about* me."

Today, we're going to blast this "judgment mentality" out of our heads!

CHANGE IT TODAY

1. **Remember, you are righteous through the blood of Jesus.** Your righteousness—or right standing with God—is not based on anything you have done or not done. Psalm 84:11 says He does not withhold one good thing from the righteous. It is impossible for God to give anything that is not good.

2. **Understand God's judgment passes over us.** God's judgment "passed over" the children of Israel through the blood of lambs. In Exodus 12:12-13 God said, "On that same night I will pass through Egypt and strike down

every firstborn—both men and animals—and I will bring judgment on all the gods of Egypt. I am the Lord. The blood will be a sign for you on the houses where you are; and when I see the blood, I will pass over you. No destructive plague will touch you when I strike Egypt," (NIV). **Today, God's judgment passes over us even more powerfully through the blood of Jesus.**

3. **Never doubt God is good and the author of good.** Every good and perfect gift comes from above, from the Father of lights (see James 1:17). God doesn't change (see Hebrews 13:8).

4. **Embrace His mercy.** Lamentations 3:22-23 says that His mercy is new every morning (NLT). Paul says in Hebrews 4:16, "So let's walk right up to Him and get what He is so ready to give. Take the mercy, accept the help," (The Message).

5. **Meditate on what mercy is.** The story is told about a woman who approached Napoleon to ask for mercy for her son and to let him go free. He was to be hanged for crimes against Napoleon and France. "Do you know what he has done, madam? He doesn't deserve mercy!" She responded: "If he deserved it, it wouldn't be mercy, sir." Napoleon released him. The next time you think "Why is this happening to me?", expect God to turn it into something good, rather than thinking God is judging you.

THINK IT & SAY IT

- I deserved judgment, but God gives me mercy!

- When things don't go right, I will not believe it's God's judgment.

- I will not believe I have lost favor with Him. His favor surrounds me like a shield.

- His judgment passed over the children of Israel, therefore His judgment passes over me.

- I expect good to happen to me. Every day, something good is going to happen.

- I embrace His mercy. It follows me all the days of my life. No matter what happens in my life, I expect God to turn it into something good!

POWER THOUGHT FOR TODAY

God is not judging me. He is my Father and He is madly in love with me.

DAY 31

"I FEEL GUILTY."

How many times have you felt this? Or maybe one of its cousin thoughts: "You don't do enough," "You're not good enough," "You don't say the right things," "You don't take care of yourself," "You don't measure up," "You don't do as much for others as you should," or "You eat too much." All this line of thinking does is produce guilt, which leads to self-hatred, anger toward others, bad decisions, harsh words, procrastination, and fear.

So often, we feel guilt because we think we don't do enough for God and for others. We think we're not good and/or holy enough. This thinking has enslaved God's people for centuries. Nothing seems to rob us of our true purpose more than thoughts and feelings of guilt.

God doesn't motivate by guilt. That's manipulation. GOD MOTIVATES BY LOVE. Romans 2:4 says, "It's the love and kindness of God that leads us to change." People will often put a guilt trip on us in order for us to act a certain way or give into them. God isn't like that. He wants you free.

Let's fast from guilt!

CHANGE IT TODAY

1. **Realize Jesus declares you:** "Not guilty!" This doesn't mean you've never done wrong. This means He washes away your wrongdoing with His blood.

2. **See what God sees.** Accept Colossians 1:22, which says through His blood, He presents you holy and faultless and unblameable in the Father's eyes.

3. **Meditate on Job 10:7.** "According to your knowledge, I am indeed not guilty."

4. **When you blow it, don't deny it.** Admit it; confess it. 1 John 1:9 says, "If you confess your sin, He is faithful and just to forgive you and to cleanse you from all unrighteousness."

5. **Believe it is already done!** Hebrews 1:3 says, "He cleansed us from our sin." It's already done!

6. **Stop thinking you have to feel "guiity" to be forgiven.** Sometimes we think we owe it to people to feel guilty and feel bad for everything. Stop thinking this way. You don't owe anyone. Guilt never pays for anything. The blood of Jesus paid it all.

7. **Stop beating yourself up about what you haven't done.** How? Live in the now. Living in the now stops your mind from bombarding you about the past and future. Enjoy each moment today—right now. When you're praying, the devil says, "You should be cleaning." When you're cleaning, the devil says, "You should be reading your Bible." Shut that garbage up! Live in the now. Hebrews 11:1 says, "*Now* faith is the substance of things hoped for." And 2 Corinthians 6:2 says, "*Now* is the time of salvation."

8. **Rest in the fact that you don't have to be perfect.** God is not holding you to a perfect standard. Jesus is your perfection. Just rest!

THINK IT & SAY IT

- I don't have to feel guilt to be forgiven and I am not going to feel guilty when I blow it.

- I will receive God's forgiveness since He already cleansed me from my sin. I will admit it, receive His mercy, and move on.

- Today, I stop beating myself up about all I haven't done or have done. I choose to live in the now. I will enjoy the moment I am in and praise God in the midst of it.

- I rest in the fact that Jesus is my perfection. I don't have to be perfect; He already is, and I put my faith in Him.

POWER THOUGHT FOR TODAY

Jesus has declared me: "Not guilty!" Even when I feel I don't do enough or I'm not good enough, God says faith in Him is enough!

DAY 32

"I DON'T DESERVE TO BE BLESSED BECAUSE OF ALL I'VE DONE WRONG."

The battles of life are won or lost between our ears. It's in our heads. Satan understands the root to everything in our lives is what we think. This is why he fights so much to fill our minds with wrong thinking. But, we have declared war on wrong thinking!

I can't be the only one who has heard this thought. The steps below take us deeper in our freedom from guilt.

CHANGE IT TODAY

1. **Stop focusing on your "wrongs," and focus on His "rights."** We've all done enough wrong in life to send us straight to hell—no passing "Go," no collecting $200.00! But God doesn't judge us based on our rights or wrongs; He judges us based on what *Jesus* did right. We just need to believe it.

2. **Remember God doesn't bless us because we deserve it.** He blesses us because He promised He would—period! This will set you free when you know God is a God of promise. The Bible says that God will bless you and multiply you, and make you exceedingly fruitful (see Genesis 17:2,6).

3. **Understand blessings flow when you believe you are forgiven.** Romans 4:7 says, "Blessed . . . are those whose sins are forgiven," (TLB). This is amazing! Putting your faith in God's forgiveness is the gateway to blessing in your life. This is why in Mark 2:1-9, Jesus said to the paralytic man whose friends lowered him through the roof, "Son, your sins are forgiven." He then said, "Take up your pallet and walk." You see, the blessing of healing was the result of believing his sins were forgiven.

4. **Acknowledge that Jesus is worthy of God's blessing, and you are in Him.** Galatians 3:29 says, "If you belong to Christ, then you are Abraham's seed, and *heirs according to the promise*," (NIV). By putting your complete faith and trust in Him, you position yourself for all God has for you. It's that simple!

5. **Stop condemning yourself.** Stop beating yourself up when you make a mistake. Romans 14:22 says, "Happy is the man who does not condemn himself," (paraphrased). God doesn't condemn you. He started a good work in you and He will finish it! (see Philippians 1:6)

6. **Recognize He took the curse so you could take the blessing!** He deserves to see you blessed because of what He went through to take your curse! "Christ redeemed us from the curse of the Law, having become a curse for us, on the cross, that the blessing of Abraham might come on us through Jesus Christ," (Galatians 3:13-14, paraphrased).

THINK IT & SAY IT

- I take my eyes off of all I have done wrong and put my eyes on all God has done right for me.

- I choose to believe I am forgiven, and therefore blessings flow.

- I belong to Christ; therefore, I am blessed with Abraham. The Bible says Abraham was blessed in all things; therefore, this is what I expect in my life (Genesis 24:1).

POWER THOUGHT FOR TODAY

God blesses me because He promised He would. I expect to be blessed coming in and blessed going out.

DAY 33

"IT'S NOT GOING TO HAPPEN FOR ME."

Have you ever had this thought? Or thoughts like: "I'm not going to get the job," "I'm not going to find the right guy or girl," or "My situation is never going to turn around." Many times in life, it seems like everyone around us is progressing and yet we are standing still. Or worse yet, going backwards. These situations breed frustration and a defeated mindset.

Today, let's begin thinking it is going to happen for us!

CHANGE IT TODAY

1. **Expect something good to happen to you today.** "The LORD has done great things for us," (Psalm 126:3).

2. **Know that God has a good plan for you today!** Jeremiah 29:11 says, "I know the plans I have for you . . . plans for good and not for evil; to give you a future and a hope," (TLB). Notice those two words: "I know." This means God is certain about it. It is definitely going to happen. You can take it to the bank! It's coming!

3. **Expect doors to open for you today.** Psalm 5:12 says that favor surrounds the righteous like a shield. "Favor" means God opens doors no one can close.

4. **Believe in God's fairness.** Life is not always fair, but God is! The Bible says He will right every wrong (see

Romans 12:19-21). Remember, it happened for Abraham, Isaac, and Jacob; therefore, it will happen for you. God is no respecter of persons (Acts 10:34, Romans 2:11). This doesn't mean He won't respect you; it means He won't show partiality by blessing one person and not another. But you have to believe it and expect it. What He did for Abraham, He has promised He will do for you. Galatians 3:29 says, "For if you belong to Christ, you are Abraham's seed, and heirs of the promise," (paraphrased).

5. **Think "solution" thoughts.** No matter what the problem is or what hasn't seemed to happen for you yet, expect a solution. Expect an answer. James 1:5-6 says, "If any of you lacks wisdom, let him ask of God, who gives to all men generously." Notice, He gives to all men, not some. You're one of those He does give it to. You're not just in line. You're in the front of the line!

6. **Think about something good that has happened in your life.** This shows the past faithfulness of God. Since He never changes, expect His faithfulness again today (Psalm 23:6).

THINK IT & SAY IT

- Something good is going to happen for me today. Things are going to work out. God has a good plan for my life today. He is certain that it is good; therefore, I'm certain as well.

- I expect favor today. Favor surrounds me like a shield. Doors are going to open for me that no one can close.

- God is going to right every wrong and show the same help to me as He did for Abraham, Isaac, and Jacob. He gives me wisdom and holds nothing back. I'm in the front of the line.

- I remember the good God has already done, and therefore I expect Him to do it again.

POWER THOUGHT FOR TODAY

Good and right things are going to happen in my life today—goodness and mercy shall follow me all the days of my life!

DAY 34

"THINGS AREN'T GETTING BETTER. THEY'RE JUST GETTING WORSE!"

You must know by now, thinking this way is not an option.

This kind of thinking keeps you bound to the past, or moving backwards. The media espouses negativity. The spirit of darkness is behind all of these thoughts. The devil promotes doom and gloom to get people depressed, on drugs, fearful and timid, distracted from the worship of God and the work of the Gospel.

The world is full of bad news: "The economy is getting worse," "Society is getting worse," etcetera, but we reject these thoughts TODAY!

Follow the pattern of how God does things. He takes us from the Old Covenant to the New Covenant; from the blood of animals to the blood of Jesus; from law to grace; from sin to righteousness; from sickness to health; from adversity to prosperity; from defeat to victory; from unclean to clean; from empty to filled.

Everything in God's Kingdom gets better and better. The Kingdom of God is in you (Luke 17:21); therefore, expect things to get better and better in every area of your life.

CHANGE IT TODAY

1. **Understand the pattern how God does things.** The path of the righteous gets brighter and brighter until the full day (Proverbs 4:18). "But we all, with open face beholding as in a glass the glory of the Lord, are changed into the same image from glory to glory, even as by the Spirit of the Lord," (2 Corinthians 3:18).

2. **Remember goodness follows you; therefore, expect to go from good to better!** "While evil men and impostors will go from bad to worse, deceiving and being deceived," (2 Timothy 3:13, NIV). But, the opposite is true about you!

3. **Don't think of the glass as "half full" or "half empty."** Instead, think: "My cup runs over!" "My cup overflows," (Psalm 23:5). This is the way God wants you to live—every day!

4. **Know your life is going to end up better than it started!** Ecclesiastes 7:8 says, "Better is the end of a thing than the beginning," (KJV). Haggai 2:9 says that the latter days of this house shall be greater than the former.

5. **Believe God has saved the best for last.** John 2:10 says, "But you have saved the best for last," (NIV, paraphrased). No matter what has happened in your life up until now—good and bad—your life is changing for the better, *From the Inside Out.*

6. **Understand God only has the best in mind for you.** In the story of the Prodigal Son, the father told his servants to bring the best robe and put it on his son (see Luke 15:22). We are the sons and daughters of God in the earth today. God only has the BEST for his kids.

THINK IT & SAY IT

- God has made me righteous through Jesus' blood; therefore, my path is getting brighter and brighter every day.

- My inner man is being renewed day by day. Evil people may go from bad to worse; but the goodness of God follows me, so I go from good to better every day.

- I can celebrate in the presence of my enemies because my cup runs over and never runs out!

- God has saved the best for last in my life, and my latter days will be better than my former days, in Jesus' Name.

POWER THOUGHT FOR TODAY

No matter what is happening in this world, things are getting better and better for me!

DAY 35

"I JUST CAN'T STOP BLOWING IT."

I f you have ever been plagued with this thought, or it's companion thought: "I always seem to mess up," then you know how frustrating this can be. The sense of failure leads to condemnation and shame, which inevitably leads to further failure and disappointment with ourselves. Feeling like you never do anything right leads to poor self-esteem and lack of confidence. I always hear parents tell their kids, "You are an accident going somewhere to happen." Then those same parents wonder why their children have such an incredibly low pictures of themselves! They become what they hear.

Jesus did more than just forgive us from our sins when He died on the cross and rose again. He gave us power over sin! No more should we see ourselves victims of a defeated, beaten life. We are the head and not the tail; above only and not beneath!

CHANGE IT TODAY

1. **Rejoice in the grace of God.** Romans 6:14 says, "For sin shall not have dominion over you. For you are not under the law, but under grace." Titus 2:11-12 says the grace of God enables us to say "no" to ungodliness.

2. **Stop beating yourself up.** Romans 14:22 says, "Happy is he who does not condemn himself." Remember, God doesn't beat you up; He builds you up. 1 Corinthians 8:1 says, "Love builds up!"

3. **Remember the woman caught in adultery.** In John 8:1-11, Jesus said to her, "I don't condemn you. Now go and sin no more." Notice, first there was acceptance and forgiveness. Then there was power over sin. The power over sin was the result of recognizing her freedom from it. Sometimes we feel we have to repent of everything before we can be forgiven. Jesus forgives first, and that gives us the power to repent and be free.

4. **Believe in the power of the blood.** Paul said not to drink the communion cup in an unworthy manner. We need to renew our mind about what makes us worthy. It's not our holiness that makes us worthy to drink the cup; it's the "cup"—the blood of Jesus which has the worthiness to cleanse us and empower us to overcome anything (see 1 Corinthians 11).

5. **Stop thinking you are out of control and realize you have been given the power of self-control.** Think about the three gifts God gives in 2 Timothy 1:7. He has not given you the spirit of fear, but of power, love, and discipline. You have the power of discipline and self-control.

THINK IT & SAY IT

- I am not a slave to sin. I have dominion over it. It doesn't have dominion over me, because I am not under the law; I'm under grace.

- I expect the free gift of God's grace to enable me to say "no" to ungodliness. I am free because I am forgiven.

- God is love and love builds me up today!

- I put my faith in the blood of Jesus to forgive me if I have fallen, but also to empower me to be free from the things I'm struggling with.

- I have the power of self-control. I am no longer out of control.

- I am free from fear and free from sin.

POWER THOUGHT FOR TODAY

I have been given power, love, and a sound mind.

DAY 36

"THAT PERSON HAS REALLY GONE TOO FAR. THEY'VE REALLY DEVASTATED ME."

Too often, we give people more power over our lives than what they actually have. By thinking they can have such a big of effect on you, you become enslaved to their whims and their attitude flavor of the month.

Over the years, I have seen numerous people live in captivity to things which had happened to them in their past. The people who hurt them have gone on with their lives, but these people carry the wounds. On some occasions, the perpetrators have already died. What this means is, these people are being ruled and hindered from the grave!

This thinking is devastating to your future and to future generations. Let's destroy these thoughts today!

CHANGE IT TODAY

1. **Fix your mind on Jesus; look at His life.** He was denied by His close disciple, Peter; betrayed by Judas; and forsaken by the rest of His disciples. He was lied about, accused, and maligned. Yet, none of it stopped Him. In fact, He used each betrayal or personal blow against Him as a path to God's greater purpose for His life.

2. **Celebrate when someone hurts you, betrays you, or accuses you.** The Bible says in 1 Corinthians 11:23, "On the same night in which He was betrayed *[while His betrayal was in progress!]* took bread," and ate it with His disciples. In Mark 14:26, he writes, "And after singing a hymn, they went out to the Mount of Olives." Jesus did not let His imminent betrayal stop Him from celebrating His Heavenly Father.

3. **See people's stumbling stones as stepping stones.** Jesus knew Judas' actions would only serve God's purpose, one way or another. Don't give people's actions permission to defeat you or hinder you. Rather, use them to step further into more of God's will.

4. **Stay attached to the promises of God's Word.** One meaning for "love" is "attached." Psalm 119:165 teaches us that anyone who loves—or stays attached to—God's Word has great peace and nothing offends them. We insulate ourselves from being offended when we love God's Word more than our feelings.

5. **Get rid of retaliation thinking.** Entrust yourself to the One who judges righteously. 1 Peter 2:23 says Jesus kept handing Himself over to God when reviled and falsely accused. When they did their worst to Him, He kept entrusting Himself into the hands of God. Do this today: entrust yourself into the hands of others as an opportunity to step further into God's will.

THINK IT & SAY IT

- I trust God will cause all things to work together for my good (Romans 8:28).

- I stay attached to what God says about it and I refuse to get offended.

- God will avenge me. I will not take vengeance or become bitter. I will continue to entrust myself to Him, as I know He will judge righteously and defend my cause!

POWER THOUGHT FOR TODAY

No matter what anyone says about me or does to me, I will not be devastated by it. I will not give them that kind of power over me.

DAY 37

"My life is out of control!"

No, it's not! That's what the devil wants you to think. He wants you to feel helpless and "under" the circumstances. When you think this way, you get discouraged. You lose hope. You give into things. Like a jellyfish, you are carried by the prevailing current.

CHANGE IT TODAY

1. **Think above.** Stop for a moment and understand what I'm saying here. Think "above," meaning, think from a higher point of view. Look "down" at life rather than "up" at it. When Elisha's servant saw from "above," he realized there were more for him than those against him (see 2 Kings 6:14-17). Notice, God didn't add any chariots. They were always there. Elisha's servant just couldn't see them because he wasn't thinking "above."

2. **Don't see the bigger picture today.** No, this is not a typo! Think of your situation and your world as small. Think of yourself bigger. Don't forget—how you see yourself is how life will see you. This is how the devil will see you, how your mountain will see you. If you see yourself bigger than the mountain and know that greater is He that is in you, then the mountain will respect what you say when you tell it to move!

3. **Decide your choices are your own; therefore, your life is your own.** No excuses. No one to blame. Remember the lame man at the pool of Bethesda? For thirty-eight years, he stayed in his condition because he told Jesus what he had believed for all those years: "I have no one to help me," (John 5:7, NIV). Decide to own your choices and you will own the life God wants you to have.

4. **Focus on the inside, not the outside.** If you're like me, there are several things on the outside which are not fully under control, but that's not my job here. My job is to get control of the inside. This is why we are FASTING FROM WRONG THINKING! It's taking care of the inside. Deal with your thoughts by continually going over these pages, these verses, and these mindsets. You are in control if you control your thought life!

5. **Take control of your day one thought at a time.** Don't get overwhelmed. Isaiah 28:13 says we build God's Word and God's thoughts in our lives, "Precept upon precept, line upon line," (NKJV).

THINK IT & SAY IT

- I am in control of my life because I am in control of my thoughts. I rule my life by ruling my thoughts. My thoughts liberate my emotions, my health, my relationships, and my whole life.

- I will think "above" beginning today. I choose to look down at life rather than look up at it. I see it from God's point of view.

- I'm bigger than my problem, bigger than the mountain, and bigger than any enemy I face today.

- Greater, larger, and more dominant is He that is in me, than he that is in the world!

- I will not stay in a defeated, lonely, sick, depressed condition another day of my life.

- I focus on the inside. I know the thoughts of victory I am developing will take care of my outside. This fast from wrong thinking is working in me, in Jesus' Name.

POWER THOUGHT FOR TODAY

Today is the best day of my life because I have control of the choices I make.

DAY 38

"WHY DON'T I HAVE MORE TIME, MONEY, SUCCESS, OR FRIENDS?"

I remember complaining to God a while back as I watched other people in my field getting blessed, getting buildings given to them, having quicker success, receiving large financial gifts into their ministries, etcetera. All the while, I was steadily plodding along, little by little. When I was done whining, I had sort of a "Solomon" moment and heard the Lord ask me this: "Would you rather have those things *or* substance and deep meaning in your relationship with Me?"

Knowing I couldn't say, "Both," I responded, of course, with the obvious answer. Then, I heard this: "Son, the things you've gone through and learned slowly are the precious secrets you have built your life upon. Now, you have something of substance to give that no one else can offer in the same way." That set me free. Then He said, "Now, the *more* will come."

I wouldn't trade the depth of relationship with God for anything in this world!

How do we fast from the thought of: "Why don't I have more?"

CHANGE IT TODAY

1. **Choose His face, rather than His hand.** The good news is: YOU WILL END UP WITH BOTH! Spend time with God. Start with a verse or these thoughts you are learning.

2. **Think positively about your adversity, rather than striving to avoid it.** Let me be clear. I am not saying adversity comes from God, but it does come. Psalm 34:19 says, "Many are the afflictions of the righteous; but the LORD delivers him out of them all." Know that adversity comes. Expect Him to deliver you. Expect to become better as a result.

3. **See your life as a gift from God and for others.** Realize your relationship with God and your life experiences have uniquely qualified you to make a difference in this world. Everyone has a motivational gift, or gifts, according to Romans 12:6-8; perhaps to show mercy or lead others through servant-hood or the gift of making money to give.

4. **Don't ever want what other people have.** King Solomon asked God to give him everything that was prescribed for him. This doesn't mean you have to settle for less than all God has for you; but don't determine what He has for you based on what other people have. God knows what He's doing in your life. The Bible says that He who began a good work in you is faithful. He will complete it until the day of His return (Philippians 1:6).

5. **Think securely.** God has reserved a place at the table for you. God told Saul not to worry about where he stood compared to others. He had prepared a place at the table and a set aside a portion especially for Saul (1 Samuel 9:23-24).

THINK IT & SAY IT

- I choose the face of God. I look positively at adversity rather than fighting to avoid it.

- I expect God to deliver me from all afflictions and trials.

- I choose to see my life as a gift from God and for others. I have a unique and special gift which will make a difference in this world.

- I know God has a portion reserved for me. He has a place for me at His table. I think securely; therefore, I live securely, in Jesus' Name.

POWER THOUGHT FOR TODAY

I won't settle for less than what God has for me, but I will not desire or covet what others have.

DAY 39

"I WONDER IF I'M DOING ENOUGH FOR GOD?"

This kind of thinking produces in us a "works" mentality and hinders the freedom and joy God wants us to experience. Christianity is not a life of attainment and achievement; it's a life of acknowledgment. This means "to recognize, appreciate, and accept."

The problem with so many Believers today is, they are striving to get God to do something for them or trying to make God's promises come to pass in their lives. You need to catch hold of three of the most important words you'll ever hear: *It's already done!*

CHANGE IT TODAY

1. **Understand everything God has is yours!** You have a covenant with Him through the blood of Jesus. The parable of the Prodigal Son is a perfect picture of us and God (see Luke 15:11-32). The father said to his son, "All that is mine is yours," (Luke 15:31).

2. **Think "blessed," not "cursed."** You are blessed, not cursed. Stop thinking since your mother or father had a disease, an anger issue, or some other problem, then you will have it, too. You have a new bloodline—the blood of Jesus. You have new DNA—the DNA of Jesus. Galatians 3:13-14 says, "Christ redeemed us from the

curse of the law, having become a curse for us on the cross. . . that the blessing of Abraham might come to us," (paraphrased).

3. **Remember: it is finished!** Ahh, the magnificent final words of Jesus on the cross! (see John 19:30). There is nothing more that has to be done for you to be saved. Nothing more has to be done for you to be accepted by God. Nothing more has to be done for you to be approved and loved! Nothing more has to be done for you to be free.

4. **Realize your job is to acknowledge and to recognize.** God has done it all. You must accept it. This is the true meaning of the word: "confess." It means "to acknowledge." We're not trying to make something happen by confessing God's Word. We're acknowledging what is already done, what is already ours. This is what brings it out of the invisible world of the spirit, into the visible world which we live. Think about the "confession of sin." When you confessed your sin is not *when* you sinned. You were simply acknowledging what was already done. When we "confess" God's promises, it's the same thing. We are acknowledging what is already done. The Bible says your faith becomes effective by acknowledging that every good thing is already in you (Philemon 6).

5. **See communion as a recognition that God is already with you, in you, and for you.** Remember in Luke 24:13-31, when the two men on the road to Emmaus thought Jesus was a stranger? When they took Him bread, it says they recognized Him. You see, He was already with them; but when they took communion, they were able to recognize and experience His presence.

THINK IT & SAY IT

- I already have a covenant with God! I'm not trying to get God to do something for me.

- I'm going to focus on believing what He has already done. This is what the Christian life is about: acknowledging what is already in us and recognizing what He has already done.

- I will live a life of acknowledgment—recognizing and praising God for what is already mine through the blood of Jesus.

- I'm blessing-conscious, rather than cursed-conscious.

- I'm connected to the blood of Jesus; therefore, I have the DNA of blessing.

- Goodness and mercy will follow me all the days of my life.

- I accept that I already have in me everything pertaining to life and godliness. I lack no good thing. It's already done! It is finished.

POWER THOUGHT FOR TODAY

I'm already blessed. I'm already healed. I'm already everything God says I am.

DAY 40

"IT'S IMPOSSIBLE!"

As we come to the close of our forty-day revolution, *From the Inside Out*, we need to take the limits off of our thinking. In order to do so, we must put aside this thought of: "It's impossible."

Jesus said, "*All things* are possible to him who believes," (Mark 9:23). What is in your life today you would consider impossible? Whatever it is (provided it's legal!), don't ever give up. NEVER, NEVER, NEVER give up!

I had an interview with the *New York Times* one year just before Easter. They asked me about racism in the Church and if it was something I was going to address on Easter Sunday. I responded, "Racism is a big story, but **SOMEONE RISING FROM THE DEAD IS EVEN BIGGER!**" The reporter didn't quite get it (go figure!) and wanted me to expound on my statement. I said, "Lady, if a man can rise from the dead, *anything is possible!*"

Let's end our forty-day revolution by destroying the thought of: "It's impossible."

CHANGE IT TODAY

1. **Think about the Resurrection of Jesus every day!** This reveals the miraculous power of God to do anything! As we meditate on this truth, we will know He can do anything He has promised.

2. **Eliminate thinking which says, "I can't believe that."** Cynicism and skepticism have filled our culture. We need to get out of the habit of questioning and doubting the possibility of things. When you think there's no way, remember, JESUS IS THE WAY (John 14:6).

3. **Deal with the real problem.** It's not whether God will help; it's whether we believe. The man with the demon-possessed son came to Jesus and said, "If you can do anything, help us," (see Mark 9:17-29). Jesus responded and said, "If you can believe," (Mark 9:23, NKJV). See, it's not whether God can do it; it's whether we can believe it. Remember, faith comes from hearing God's Word (Romans 10:17).

4. **Believe your words move mountains.** Matthew 17:20 says, "You shall say to this mountain, 'Move from here to there,' and it shall move; and nothing shall be impossible to you."

5. **Meditate on people who had an impossible situation turn around.** Abraham was ninety-nine years old when he had a son. Sarah was ninety. Moses parted the Red Sea, and the list goes on and on. Find those people in the Bible and fill your mind with their testimonies. Hebrews 12:1 says that we have a great cloud of witnesses surrounding us. If it could happen for them, it can happen for you, and IT WILL. Don't throw away your confidence in God's promises because the Bible says, "It is impossible for God to lie," (Hebrews 6:18).

THINK IT & SAY IT

- Since Jesus arose from the dead, anything is possible.

- I expect impossible situations to become possible— TODAY!

- I now say, "I CAN believe that!"

- Jesus will make a way where there seems to be no way.

- I believe God can and will do anything in His Word that I believe. Since my words can move mountains, nothing will be impossible for me.

- I will not throw away my confidence in God's Word because it is impossible for God to lie!

POWER THOUGHT FOR TODAY

All of God's promises WILL happen in my life—beginning today!

CONCLUSION

Now that you've begun this revolution, *From the Inside Out*, let me encourage you with a few final thoughts:

1. **Review regularly**. Don't be fooled. The devil will try to make you fall back into wrong thinking. Whenever a negative thought comes back, go back and review how to overcome this thought from that particular day.

2. **Read your journal**. One of the quickest ways to avoid reverting into a negative thought is to read what YOU wrote during this fast from wrong thinking. Remind yourself of what God spoke to you directly.

3. **Share your testimony**. Something else that will keep you walking in victory is sharing how God has changed your life! Please send me your testimony at www.thinkingfast.org. You can help someone else know their life can be changed, too!

4. **Help me change the world.** God has called us to change the world, *From the Inside Out,* by changing the way we think! This is a big job, but just remember, our thought from Day 40—NOTHING IS IMPOSSIBLE. You can help take this revolutionary message to millions of others around the world by sowing a seed of any amount. Just log onto www.thinkingfast.org and click on "Make a Donation." Stand with me in getting the word out about this life-changing fast from wrong thinking.

5. **Finally, don't ever forget!** There is no stopping the man or woman who is set free from wrong thinking! Remember, "As a man thinks within, so is he!" (Proverbs 23:7).

More Products Available From Gregory Dickow

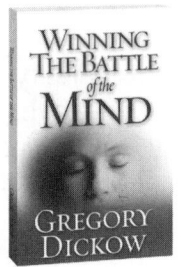

Winning the Battle of the Mind Book

The devil has been defeated! Jesus is Lord! So why do so many people still struggle? The answer is right between our ears! Our thinking   paves the way for victory or defeat in our lives.

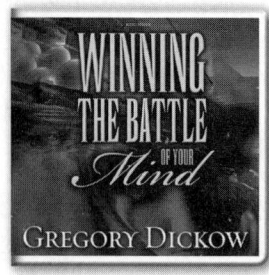

Winning the Battle of Your Mind
5-CD Series

In this powerful teaching, Gregory Dickow will teach you how to get rid of habits and change your behavior by learning to think the right thoughts. Take charge of your life today by taking control of your thinking!

Mind Games
3-CD Series

Stop playing games with your life and destiny! The quality of life you are experiencing right now is the direct result of your thought life. Gregory Dickow shows you how to take control of the outcome of your life. Find out how to change the way you think, take every thought captive, and win the battle of the mind.

CONQUERING YOUR FLESH BOOK

It's not as hard as you may think! Discover how to experience all of God's blessings for your life, and learn the surprising definition of what your "flesh" really is. Gregory Dickow also shows how to simply and completely deal with your flesh—which is the key to stopping the cycle of failure in your life—and how to consistently walk in the spirit. Begin experiencing the freedom you've always wanted by *conquering your flesh*!

FLESH, YOU'RE FIRED 5-CD SERIES

In this powerful series, Pastor Dickow will equip you with the understanding you need to stop being controlled by your flesh and begin winning over it. Learn how to walk in the spirit, and begin removing the limits that have been holding you back! If you are ready to start experiencing the freedom you've always wanted, this teaching is for you!

BREAKING THE POWER OF INFERIORITY — BOOK

Pastor Gregory Dickow reveals Biblical solutions to being free from inferiority and becoming all God intended you to be. Learn the signs of inferiority, how to break the cycle of insecurity, the difference between dominion & domination, one word that destroys inferiority, the solution to jealousy, how to reign in life as a king, and much more!

FROM THE INSIDE OUT 5-CD SERIES

We all want to change something in our lives. But the reason so many people don't see lasting change is because they're trying to change on the outside. You don't have to stay the way you are; but you won't change just because you make a decision to change! You must have the right knowledge to change your way of thinking. When you change your thinking, you will change your life. Let Gregory Dickow show you the simple steps to lasting change—*From the Inside Out*.

FOR MORE INFORMATION AND
RESOURCES FROM GREGORY DICKOW,
PLEASE CONTACT:

GREGORY DICKOW MINISTRIES
P.O. BOX 7000
CHICAGO, IL 60680

888.849.5433

www.gregorydickow.org

www.thinkingfast.org

gdm
GREGORY DICKOW MINISTRIES